Bruce Haley

HOME FIRES

Vol. I: The Past

Daylight

Cofounders: Taj Forer and Michael Itkoff
Art Director: Ursula Damm
Copy Editor: Gabrielle Fastman

© 2020 Daylight Community Arts Foundation

Photographs © 2014 by Bruce Haley

"Introduction" © 2020 by Bruce Haley
"Genetics of Place" © 2020 by Kirsten Rian

All rights reserved.

ISBN: 978-1-942084-88-4

Printed by OFSET YAPIMEVI, Turkey

Daylight Books
E-mail: info@daylightbooks.org
Web: www.daylightbooks.org

INTRODUCTION

by Bruce Haley

THE CHILD

I remember the fish and the desperation.

As the water evaporated, scores of them would be forced into small, shallow, muddy puddles. Even from a distance you could see the frenzy—mouths, tail fins, dorsal fins, pectoral fins, visible above the surface, all pressed together, frantic, flipping and writhing and glistening in the intense heat of a San Joaquin Valley summer afternoon.

If they were lucky, someone somewhere—whoever controlled the water—would open up the flow before the puddles dried completely; in most cases this last-minute reprieve never arrived.

As a ten-year-old I wouldn't have known the term "riparian zone," but in retrospect I understand and appreciate the vital role that several such areas played in my life. They fueled my boyhood imagination and my need to explore, and provided refuge and solace from events in my everyday life that were beyond my control.

The South Fork of the Kings River arced around our property. In reality it was little more than a glorified irrigation ditch, existing solely to deliver water to farmers (everyone in the area referred to it simply as "the canal"), but it had rushes and cattails and the banks had trees and were overgrown with bushes and brambles and weeds. A short distance upstream there was a small weir. In a matter of minutes I could leave the house, cross the back pasture past the huge Valley oak, climb the small levee, slip between the strands of a barbed wire fence, and be all alone in my private riparian sanctuary.

Even better, about half a mile away (as the crow flies) was my "wilderness" place, big to the eyes of a boy, full of mystery and ripe for exploration, where glimpses of owls and possums and foxes were possible. Tangled, forgotten, untouched—it was a rare tract of land even then, a relic in an area where most every piece of ground was made productive.

To get to my wild place, I had to follow dirt roads past fields of cotton or alfalfa or corn, and then pass through a walnut orchard and along a concrete-lined irrigation ditch. From there I would cross an overgrown field that still bore the telltale signs of previous cultivation, and only then would I have arrived in my wilderness.

Growing up in an agricultural area, property and boundaries are everything—and the demarcations are seared into your psyche. With each step along the way I would be conscious of whose property I was walking through: here is Fagundes land, then Roberts land, Brown land, Stone land. I was never certain who owned my forgotten place, but its days were already numbered and it didn't survive much past my childhood.

Nothing lasts. Puddles evaporate and every single gasping fish dies. I grew up and moved on, gone like those wild creatures in my relic wilderness that were driven before the tractor and the harrow.

THE OKIES

There is an old photograph, taken circa 1900, of the Haley homestead in Lincoln County, Oklahoma. It shows my great-grandparents and several of their nine children, along with a few horses and cows and a dog. They were living in a dugout, while a few of the kids were relegated to a canvas tent.

My father was born eighteen years after that photograph was taken. He was one of eight children, and they were still in Oklahoma. I never knew either of my Haley grandparents; my grandmother Nancy died at the age of 38, a kind and sweet woman who was "plumb wore out."

My father and his family were part of the "Okie migration" to California, but they came in the 1920s, prior to the Depression and the Dust Bowl. I'm led to believe, however, that in their case the desperation was similar.

The route would become well-worn: from Oklahoma through the Texas Panhandle, then on through New Mexico and Arizona, and finally into California. This would become the legendary Route 66, although the "kicks" mentioned in the famous song would have to wait until later.

The Haley family followed the trail of the migrant labor camps and eventually ended up in the San Joaquin Valley. My father would be raised by an older sister and her husband in Kingsburg. To help ease their financial burden he dropped out of high school to join the Army, and that took him out of the Valley. It would be over thirty years before he lived there again.

There is a much-quoted scene in John Steinbeck's *The Grapes of Wrath* where the Joad family first glimpses the San Joaquin Valley. Coming down off of the Tehachapi Pass, they pull their truck to the side of the road and get out for a better look—before them they see only hope and plenty.

The parallels between the fictional Joads and the real Haleys are obvious. I often wonder if my family did something similar, or had those same thoughts upon first entering the Valley. Was the young child who would become my father swept away with visions and dreams of a better future? And how long did it take for those dreams to become tempered by reality?

THE DROUGHT

Hard times may come and go, but mostly it seems they just stick around and fluctuate in severity.

In January of 2014, California Governor Jerry Brown declared a drought state of emergency, citing "conditions of extreme peril to the safety of persons and property."

The San Joaquin Valley was hit particularly hard—crops and orchards and dairies were lost, and the old saying "whiskey is for drinking and water is for fighting" rang strikingly true. Fractures occurred along the usual political fault lines—farmers versus environmentalists, urban versus rural—and a tiny fish that smells like cucumber became the prism through which a myriad of complex issues were examined and contested.

The photographs in this book were taken during the height of this historic drought. In addition, they were all taken during winter, when the hectic activities of the agriculture industry are absent: no crops, no crop dusters swooping overhead, no tractors, no swathers, no balers, no lines of laborers bent over in shimmering heat.

You are seeing the bare bones of winter compounded by the skeletal effects of an epic drought, underpinned by memory and the ghosts of childhood lost.

Before you turn the page, imagine that you're driving a '77 Ford F-150 (with lift kit, roll bar and fog lights, of course) past the nodding derricks of the Midway-Sunset oil fields. Merle Haggard, the poet laureate of the San Joaquin Valley, raised in a converted boxcar in Oildale, is playing on an 8-track tape blaring out of tinny Kraco speakers. You have one eye on the rearview, one eye on Highway 33, and your mind's eye on an uncertain future.

But mostly you're looking in that rearview because you have an open Coors longneck in your hand.

Okies, Merle, memory.

The San Joaquin.

Water.

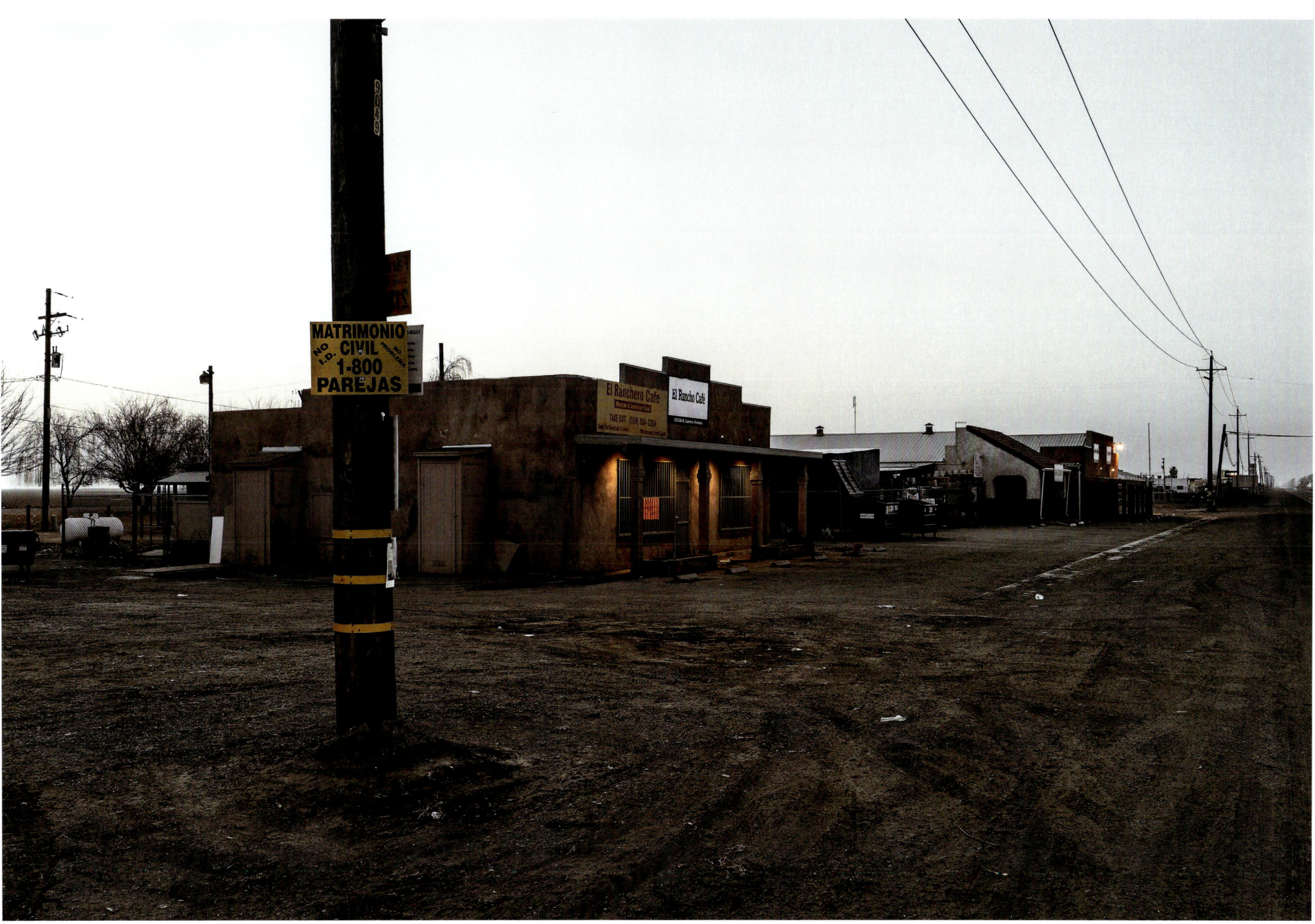

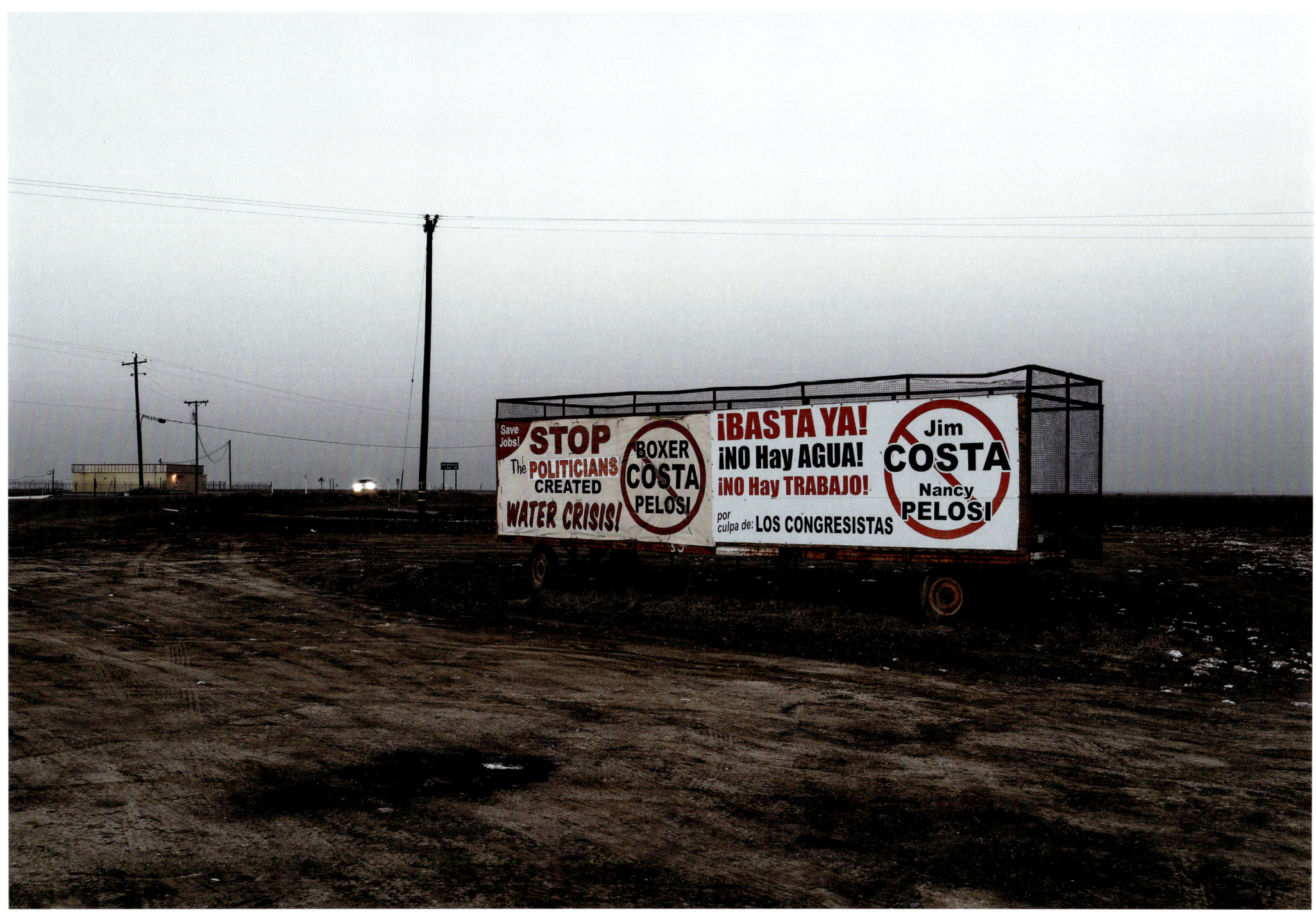

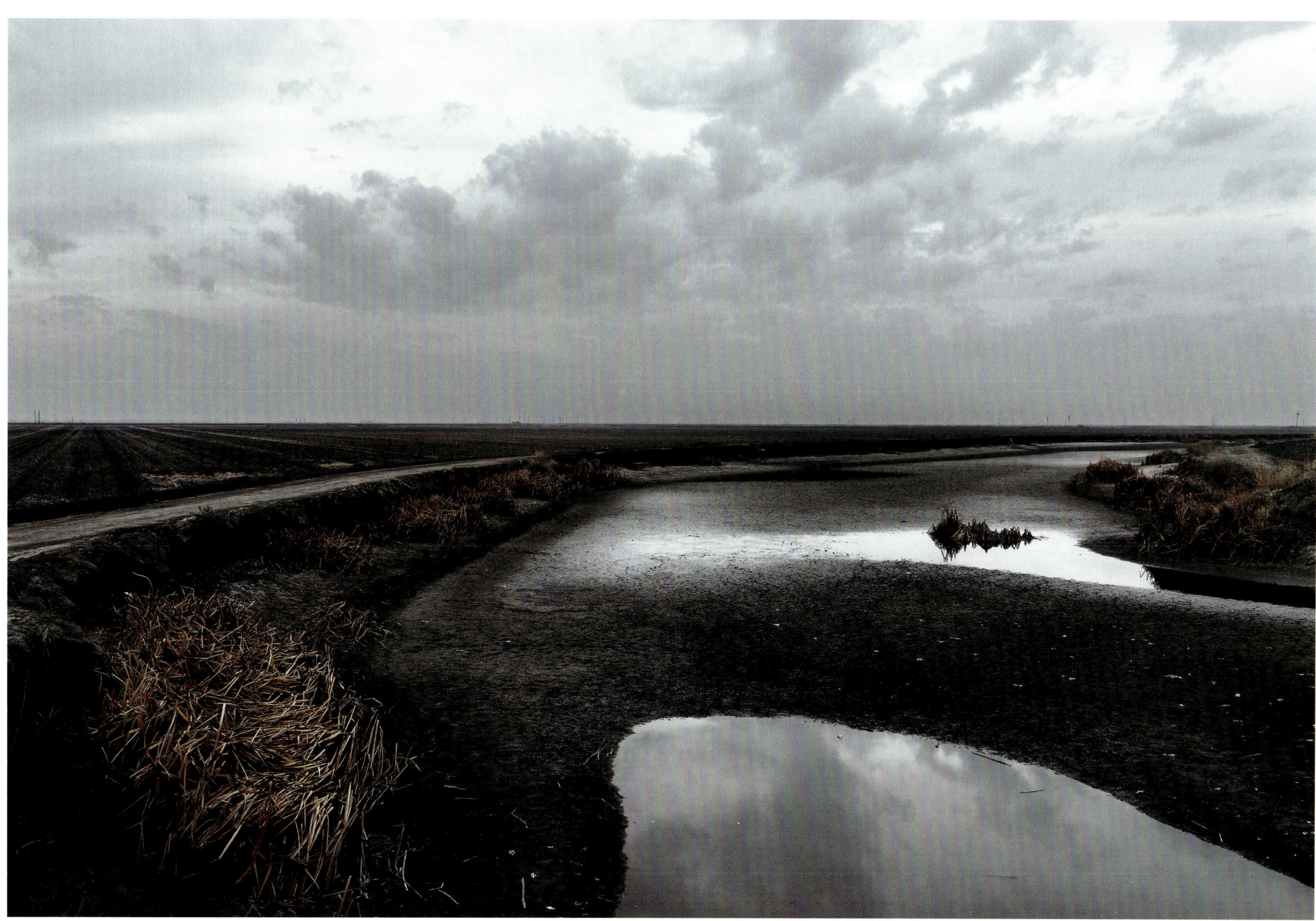

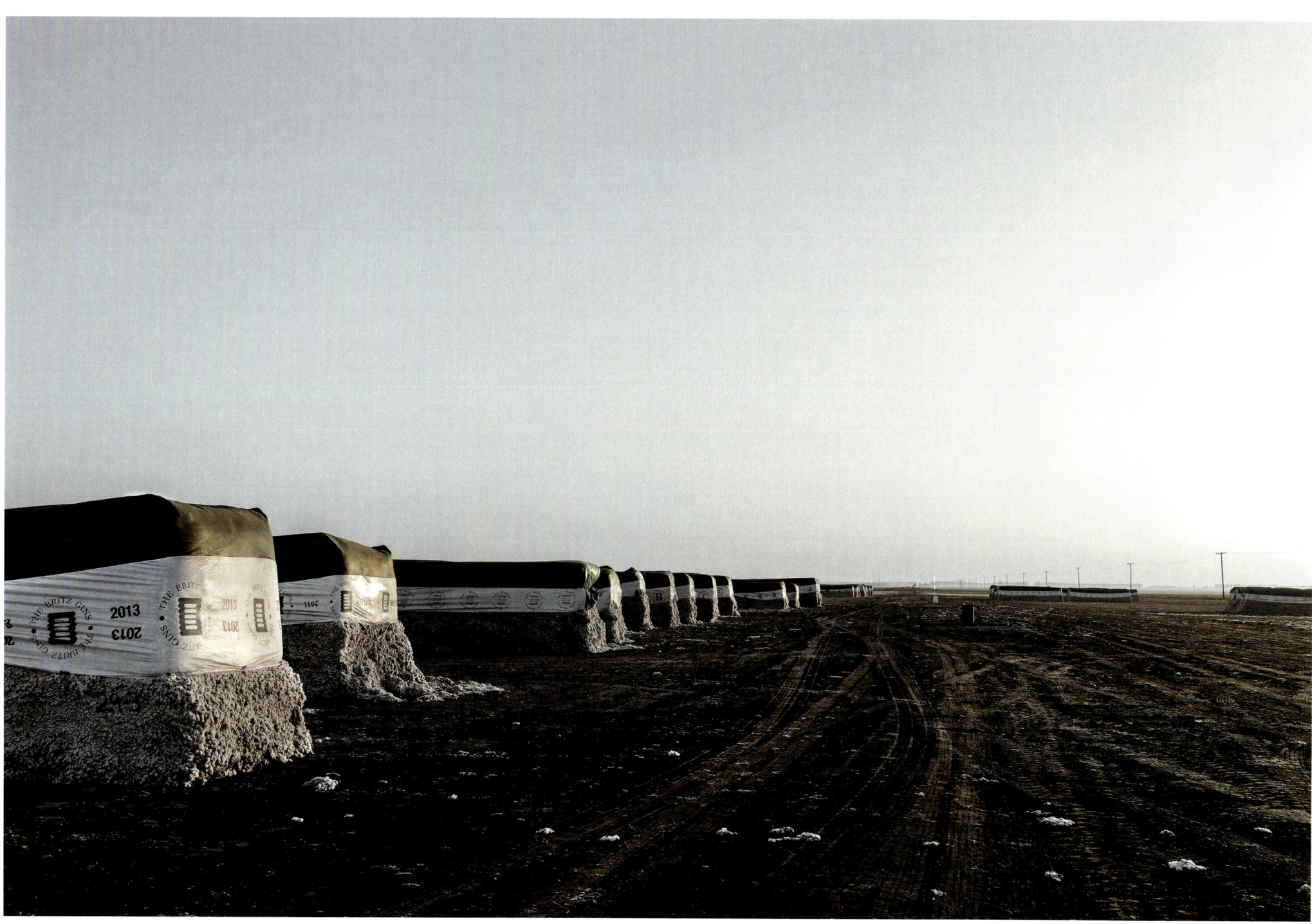

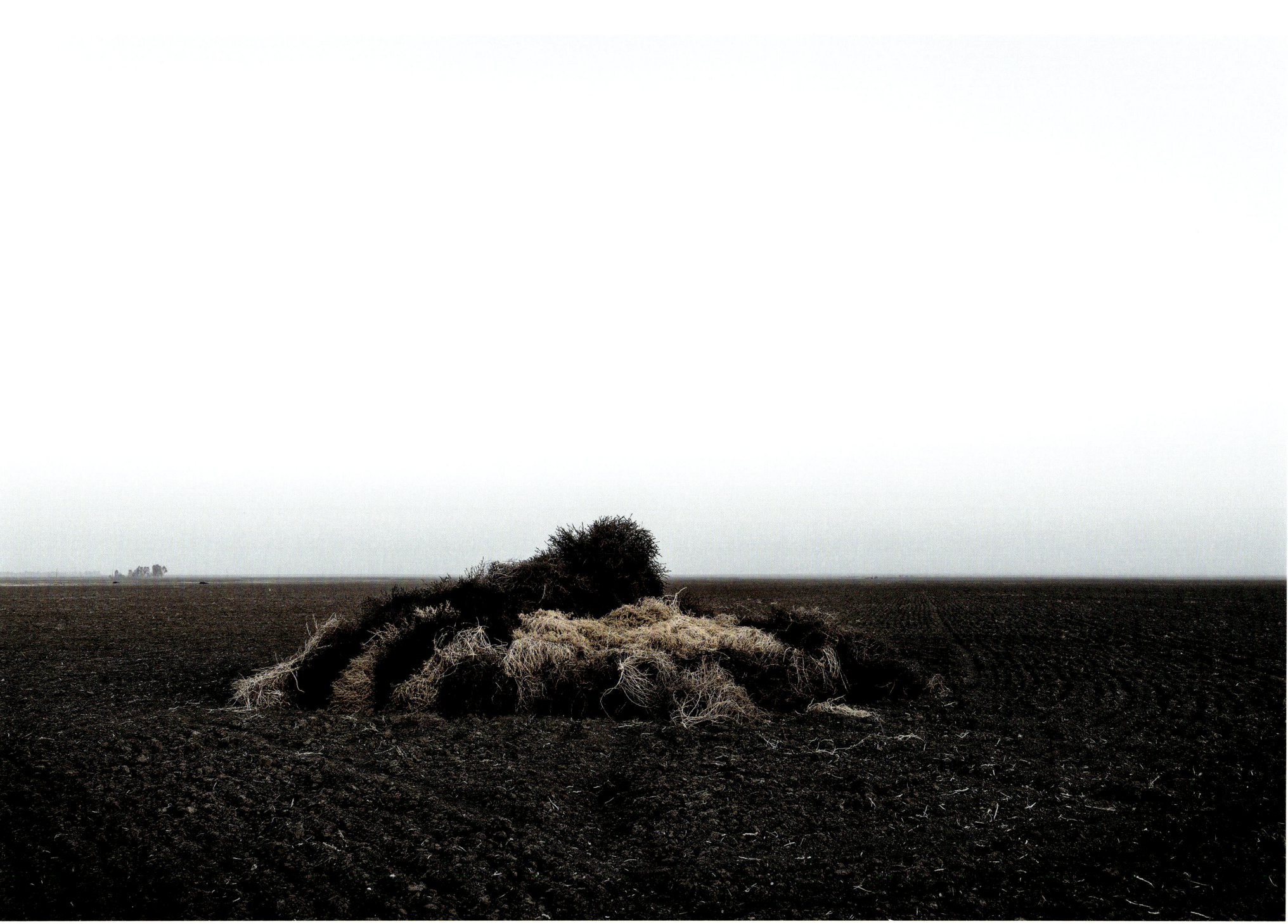

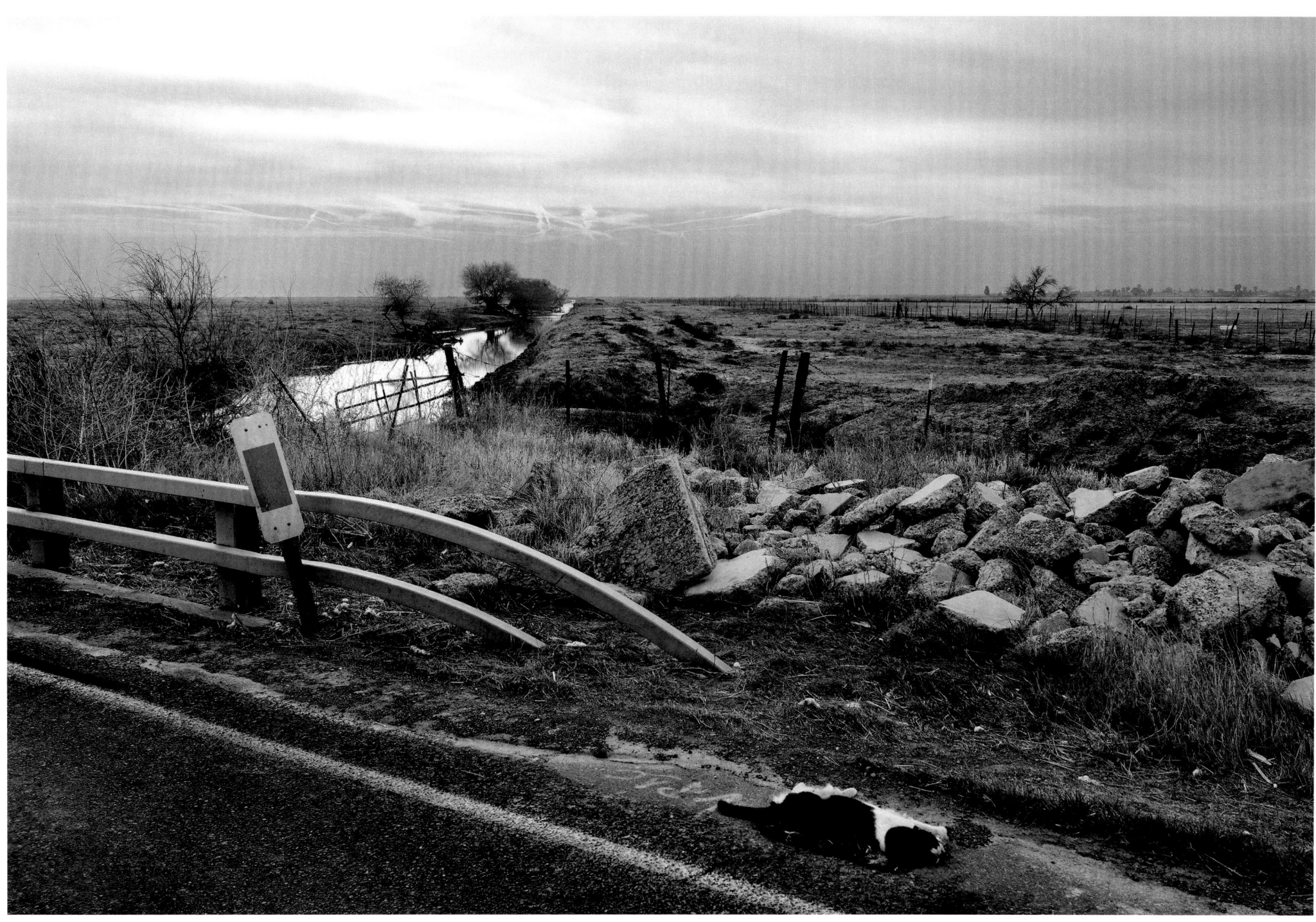

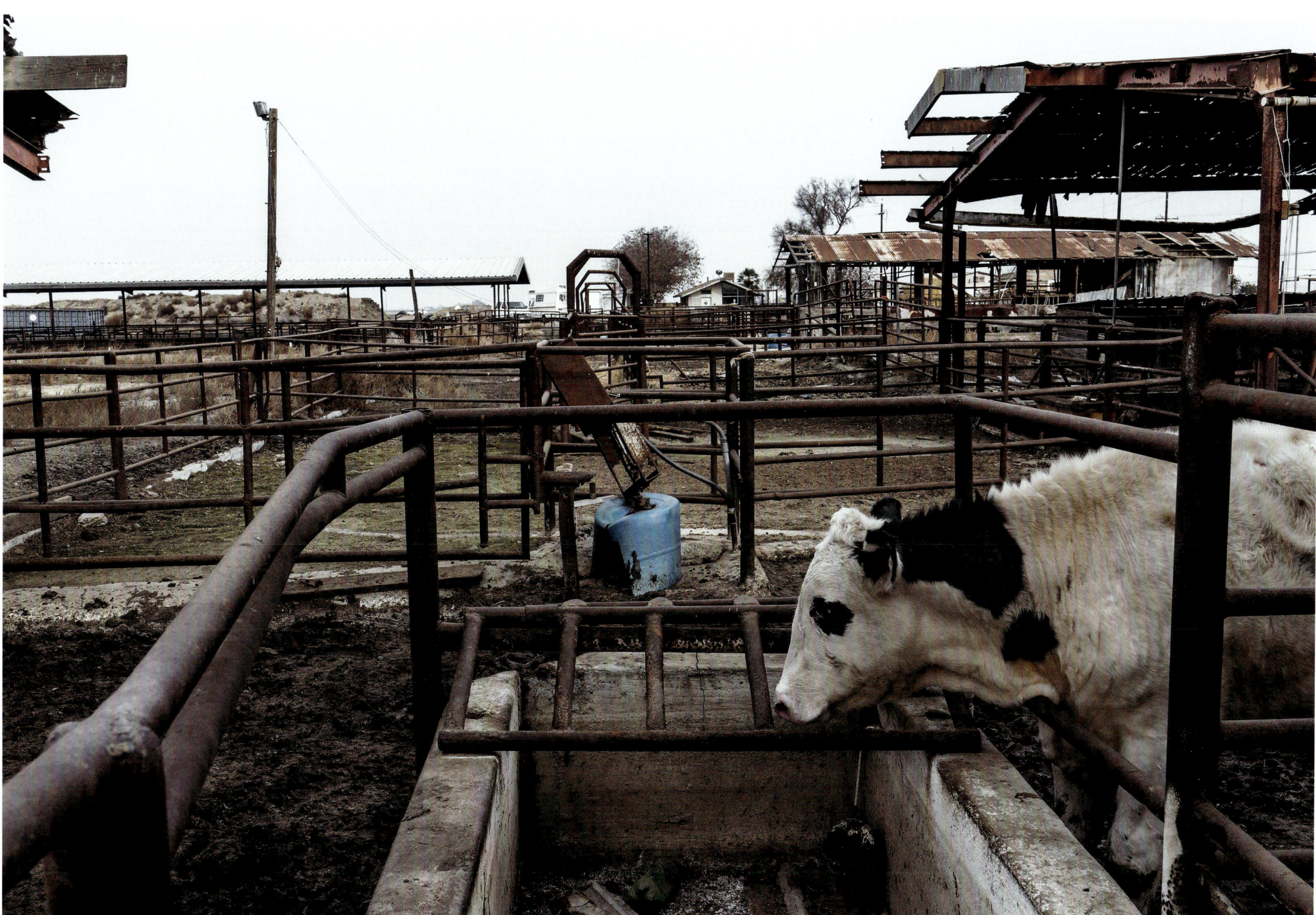

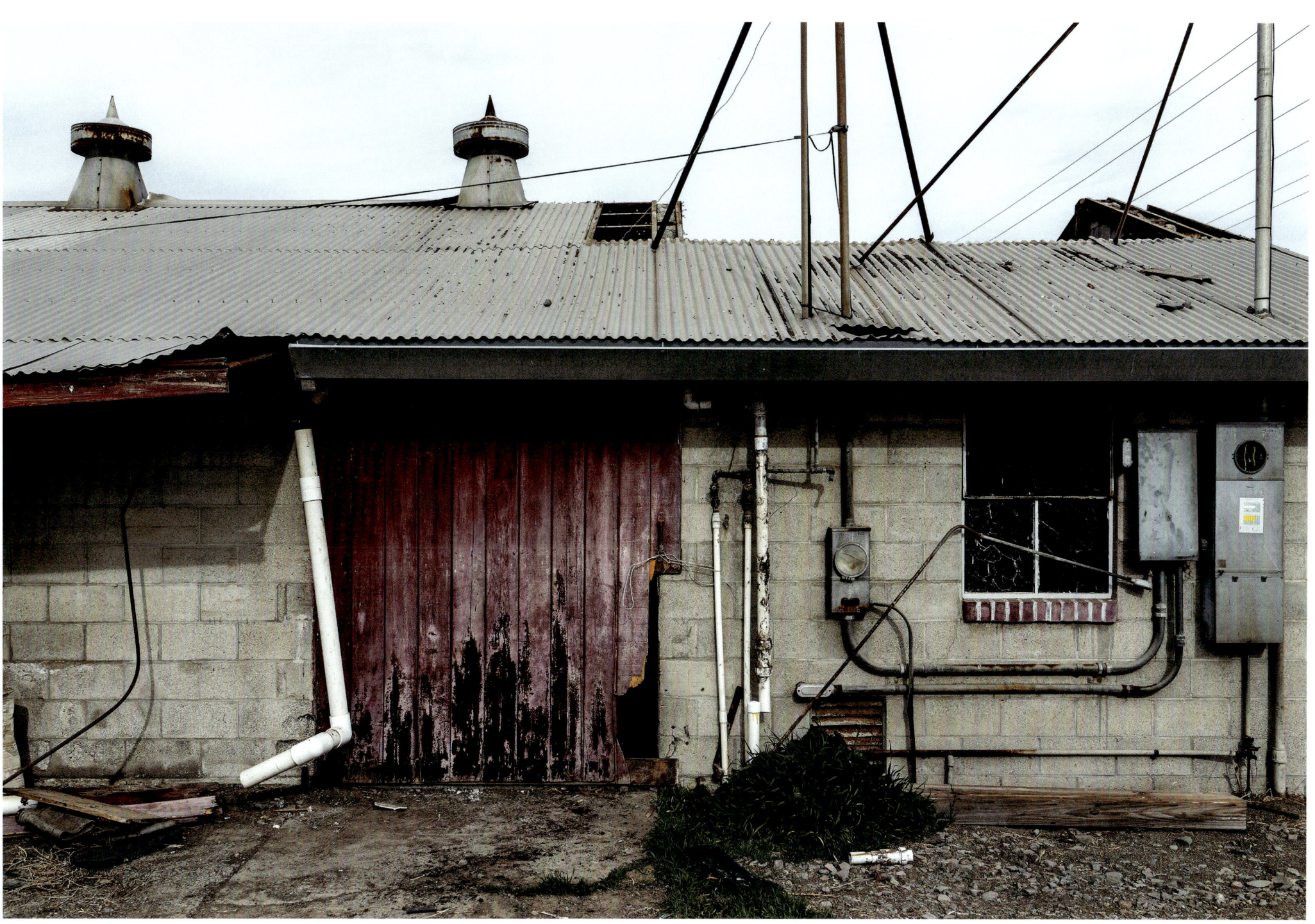

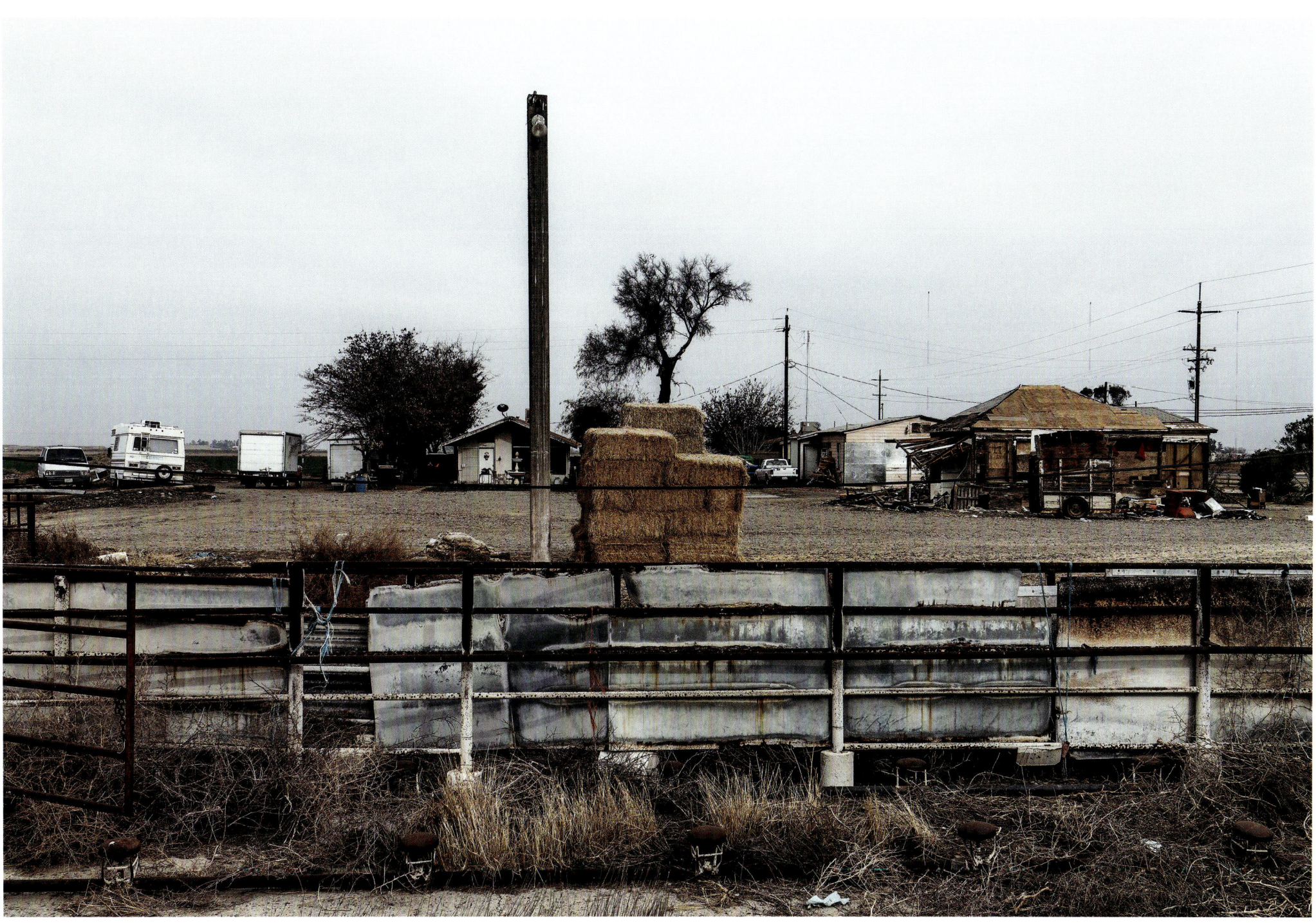

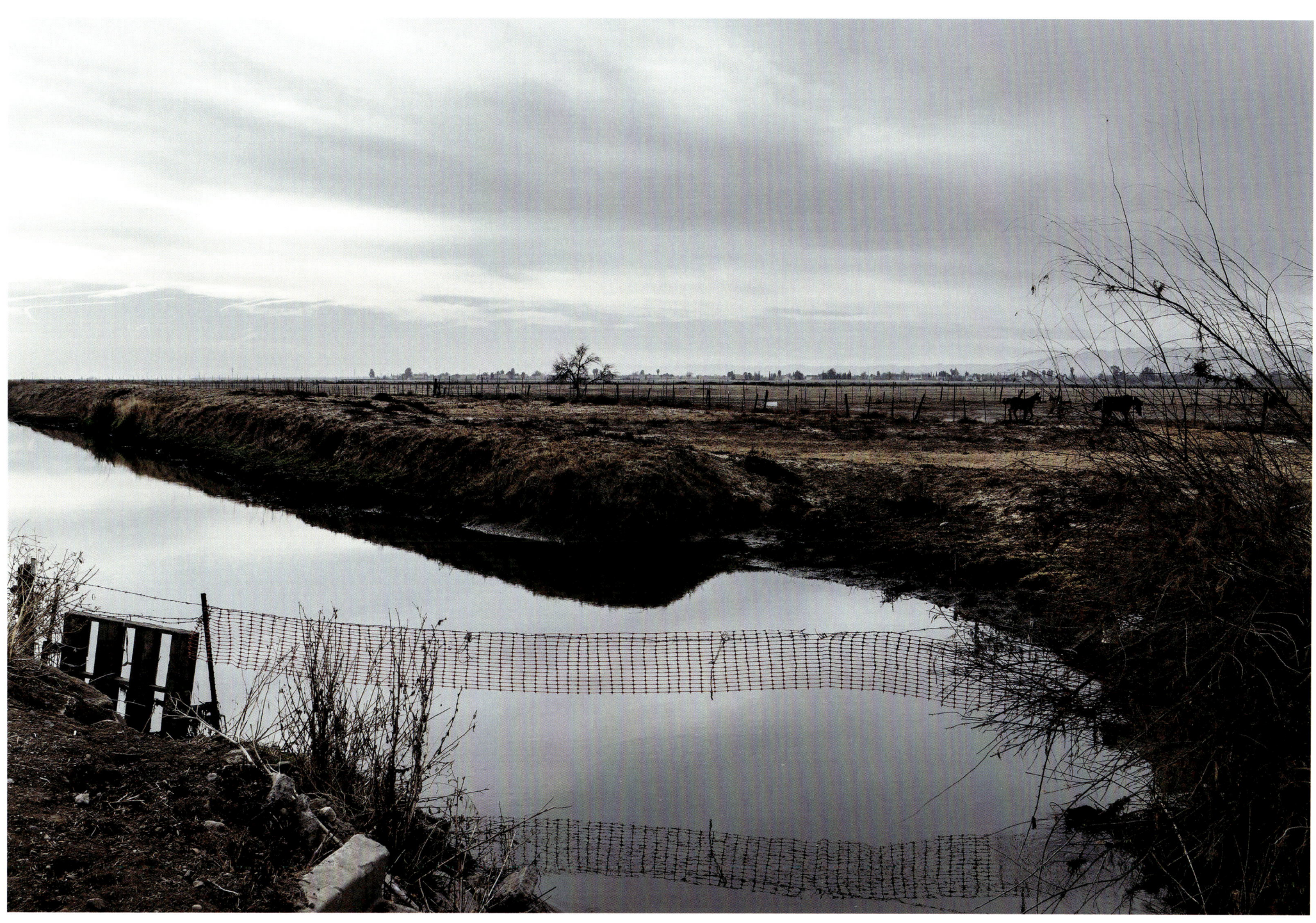

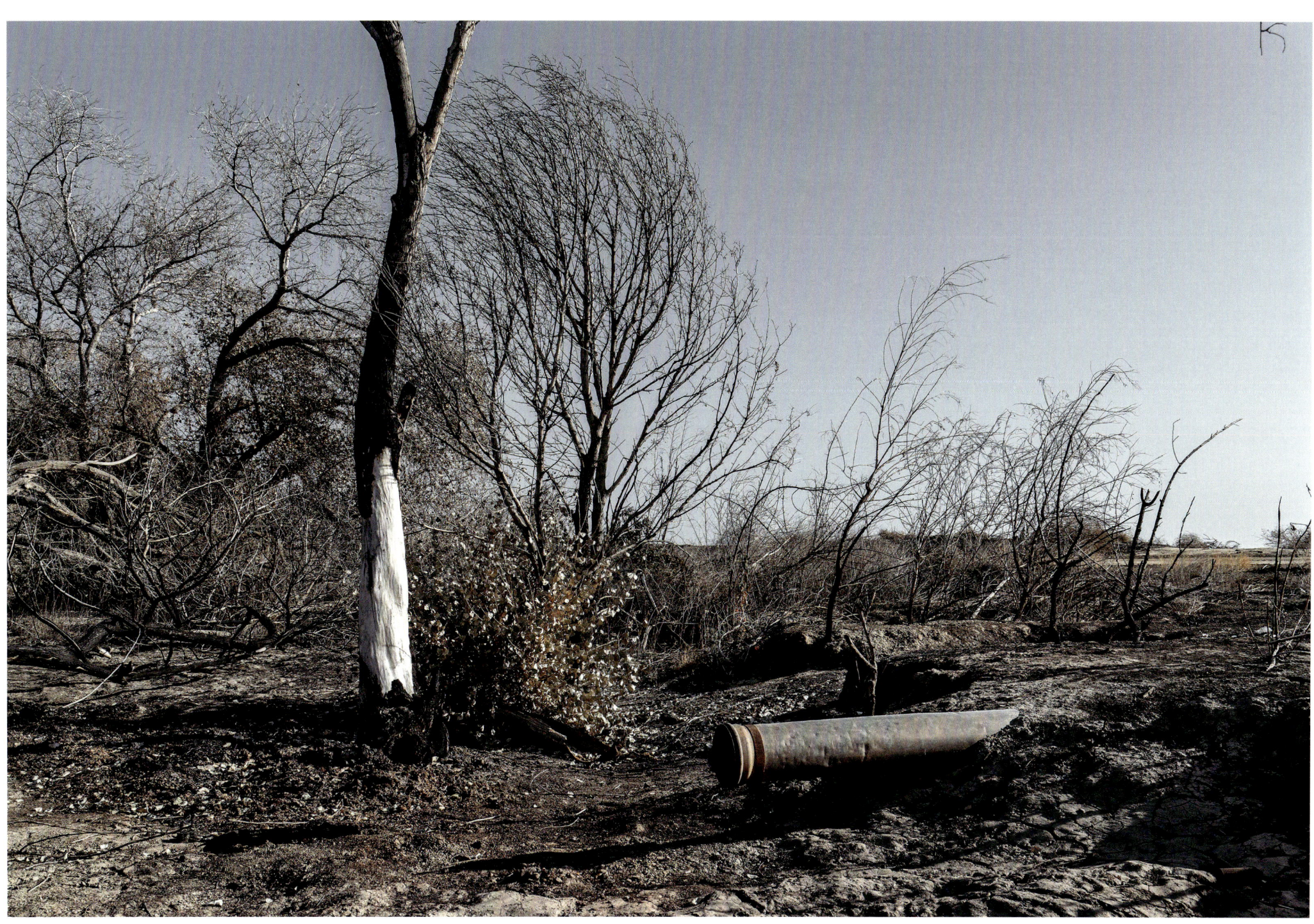

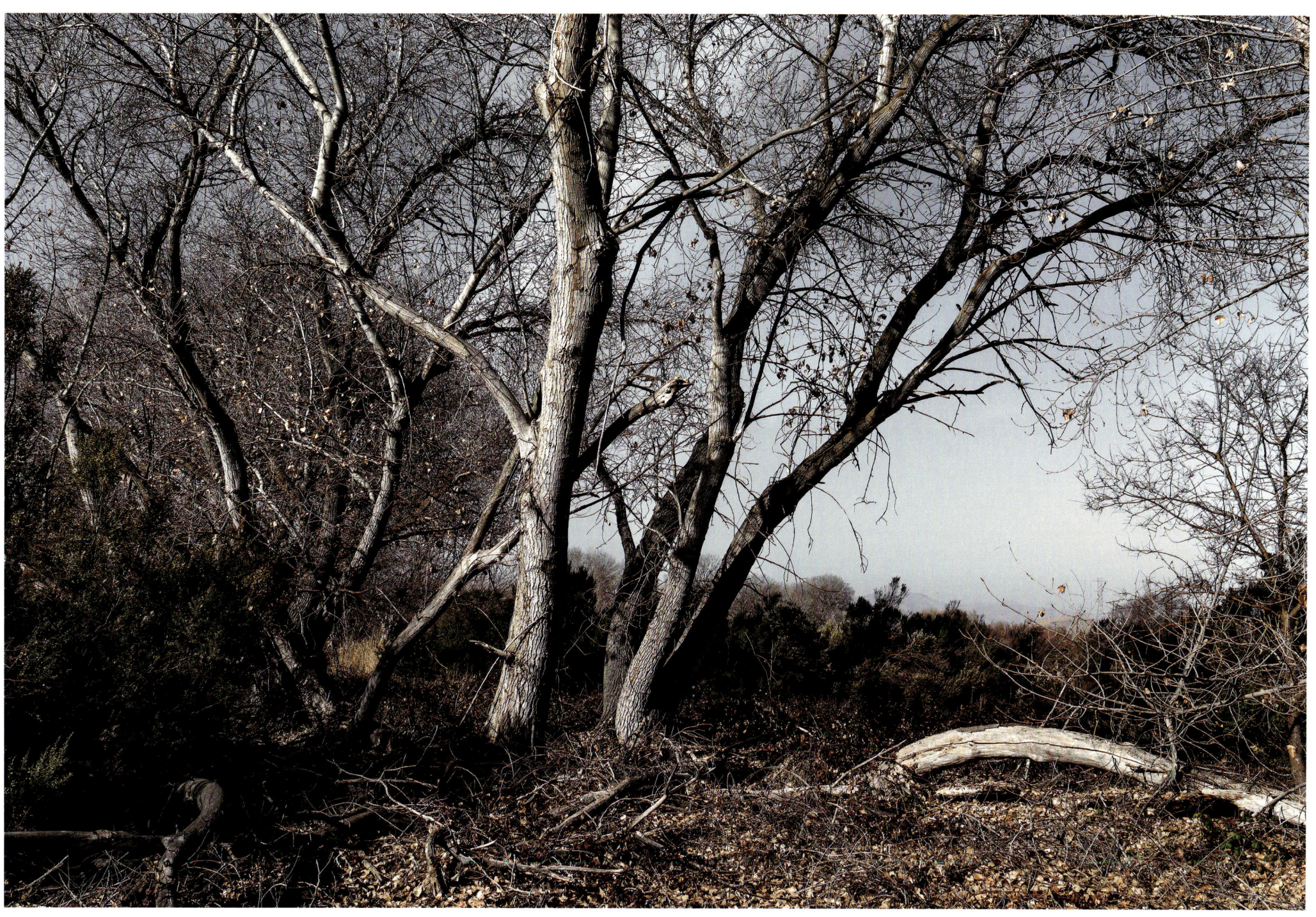

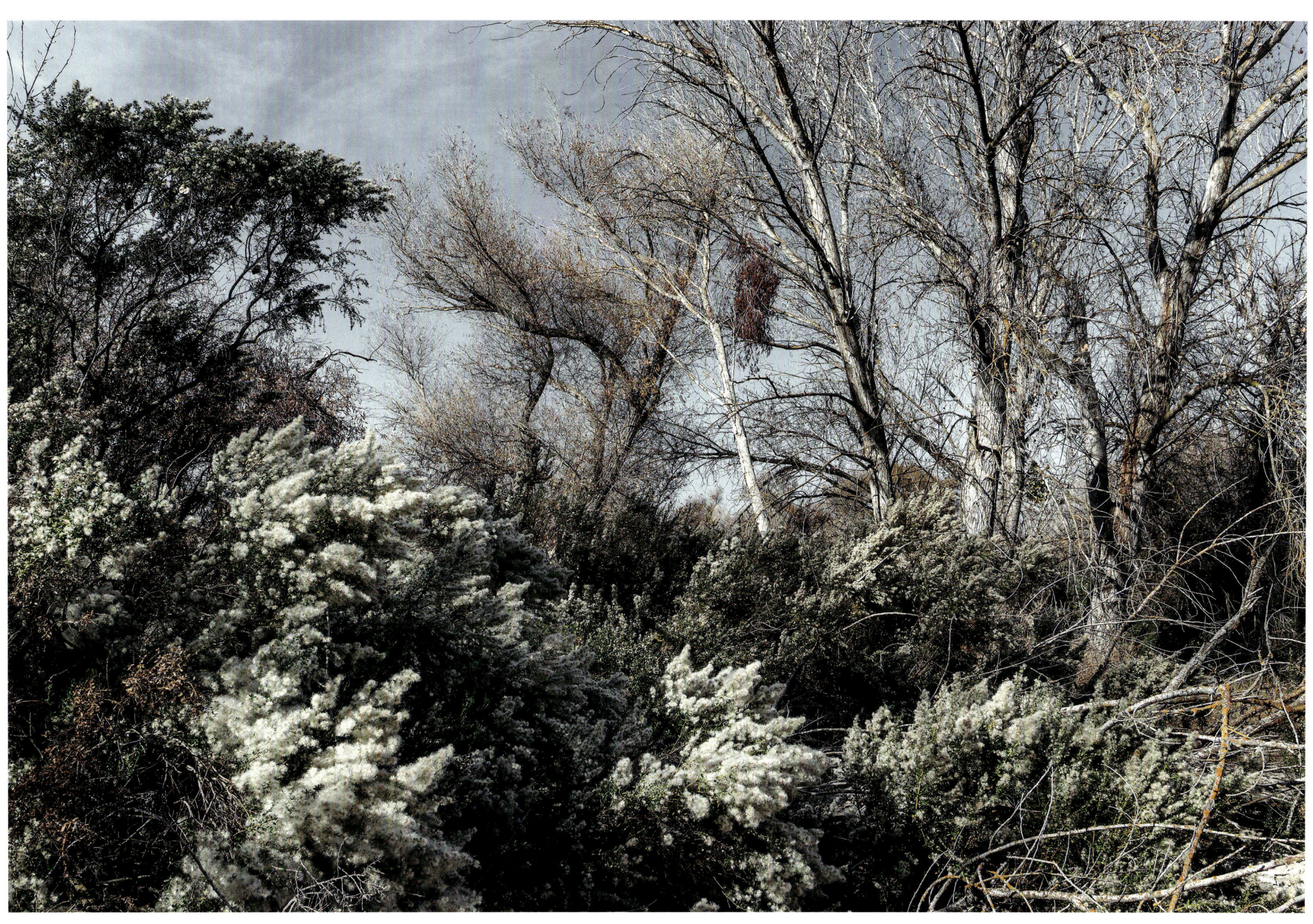

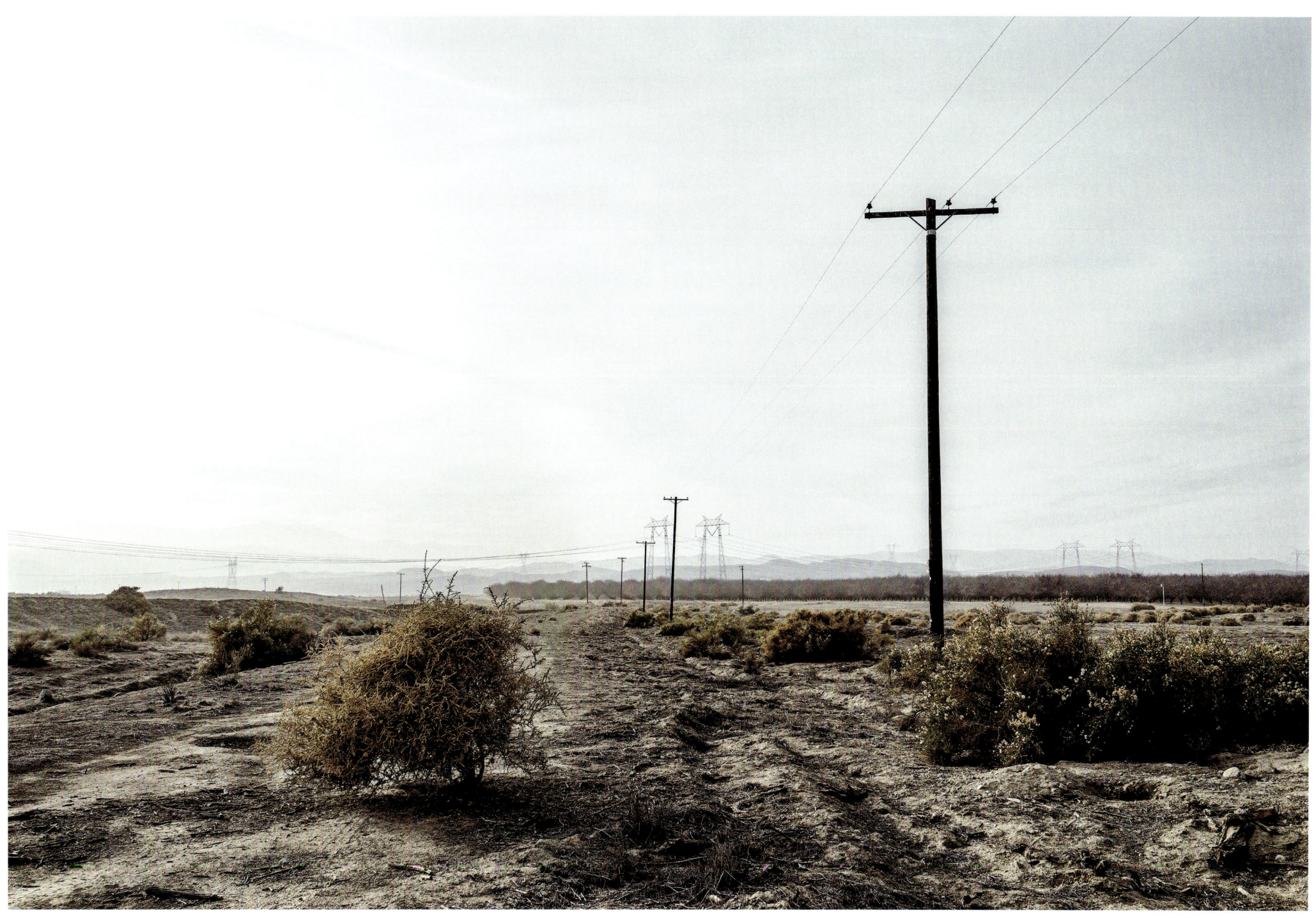

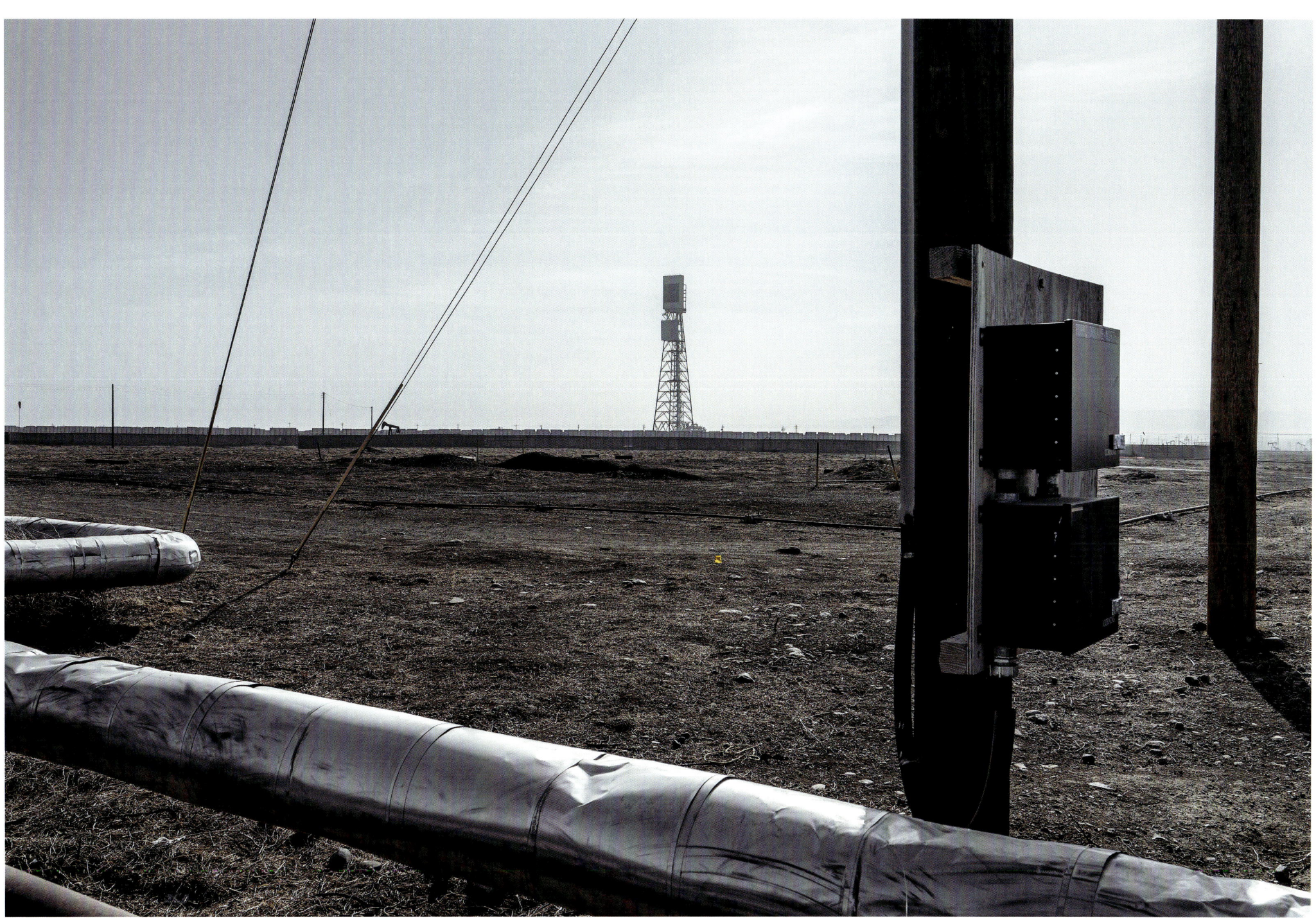

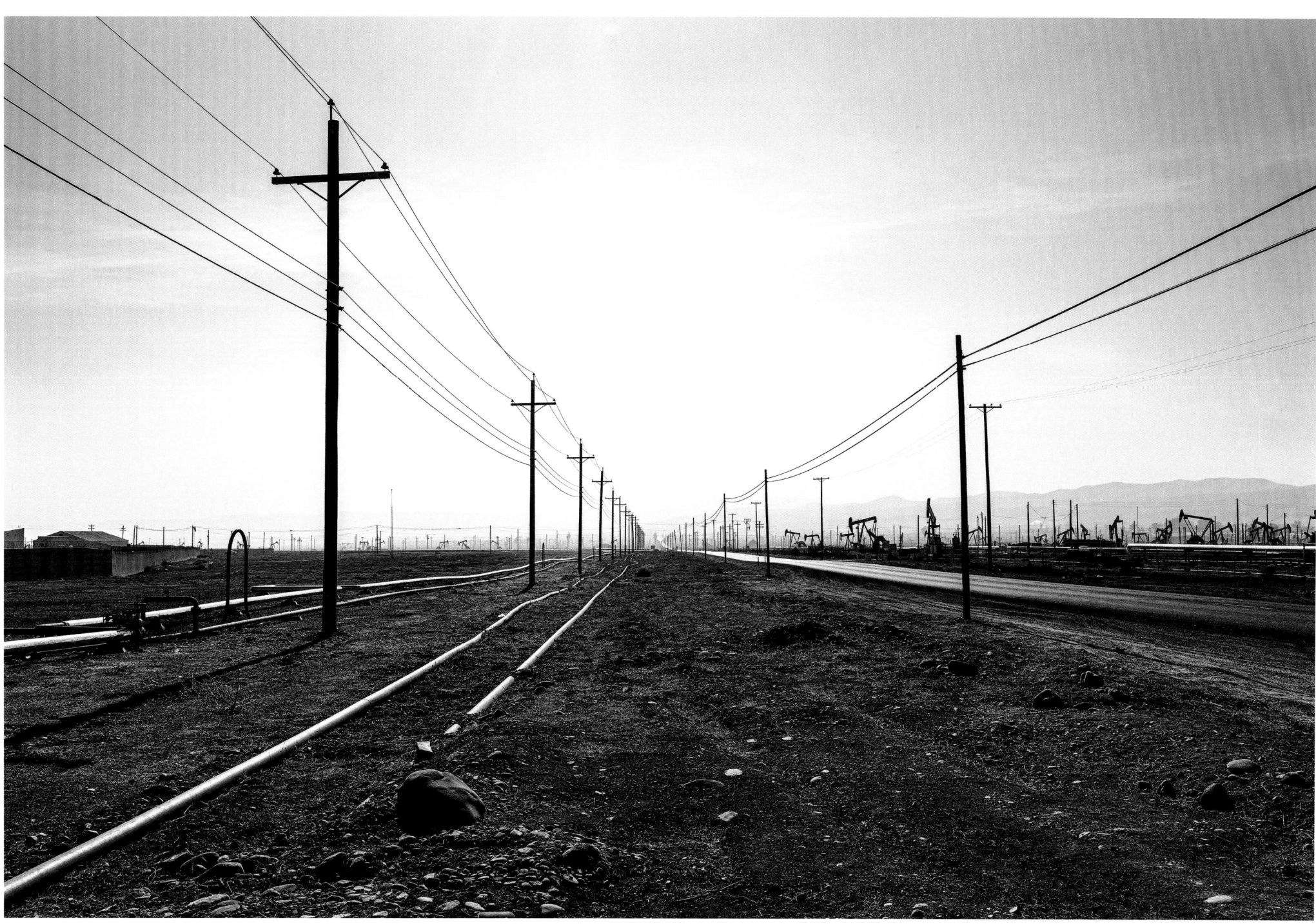

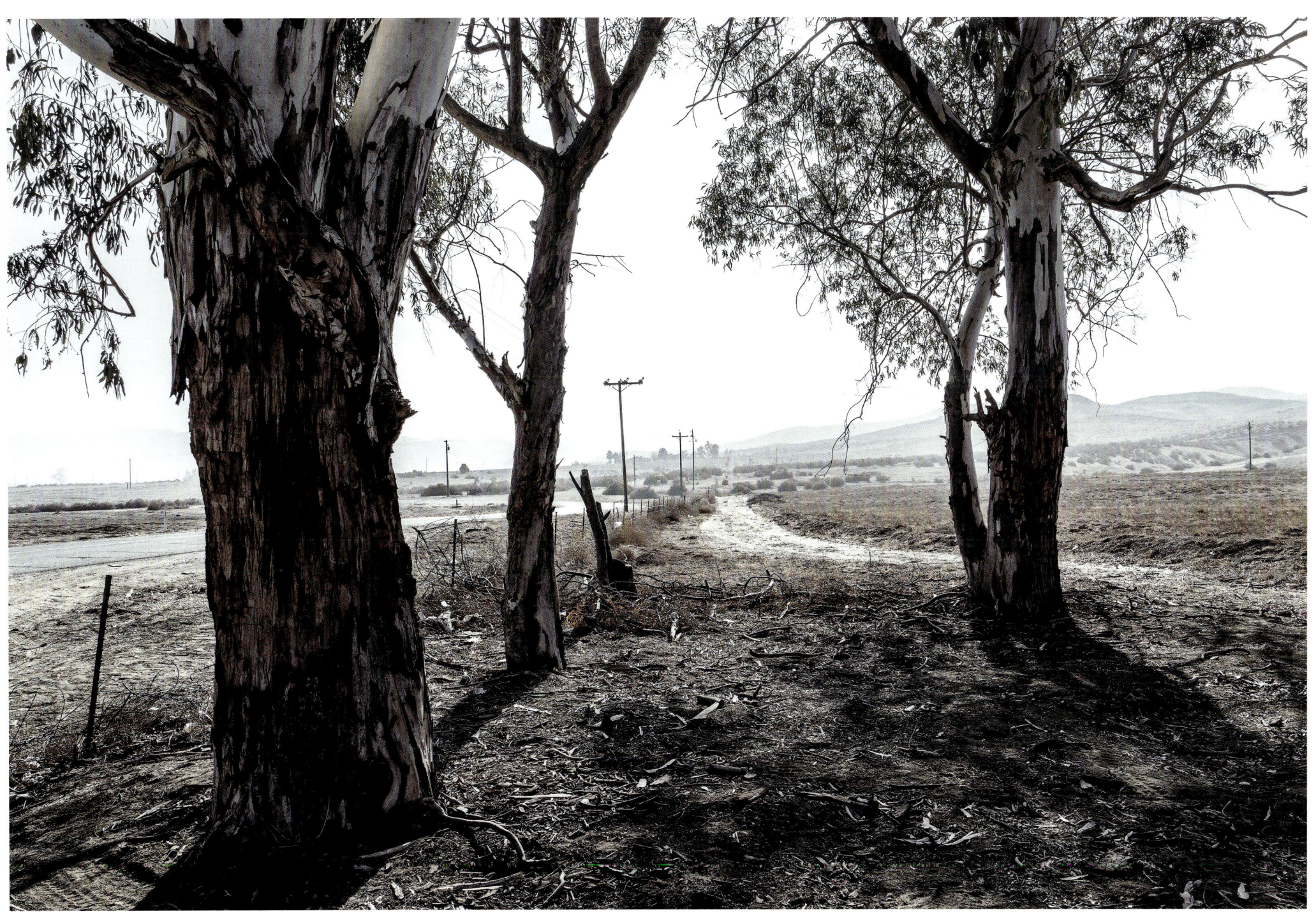

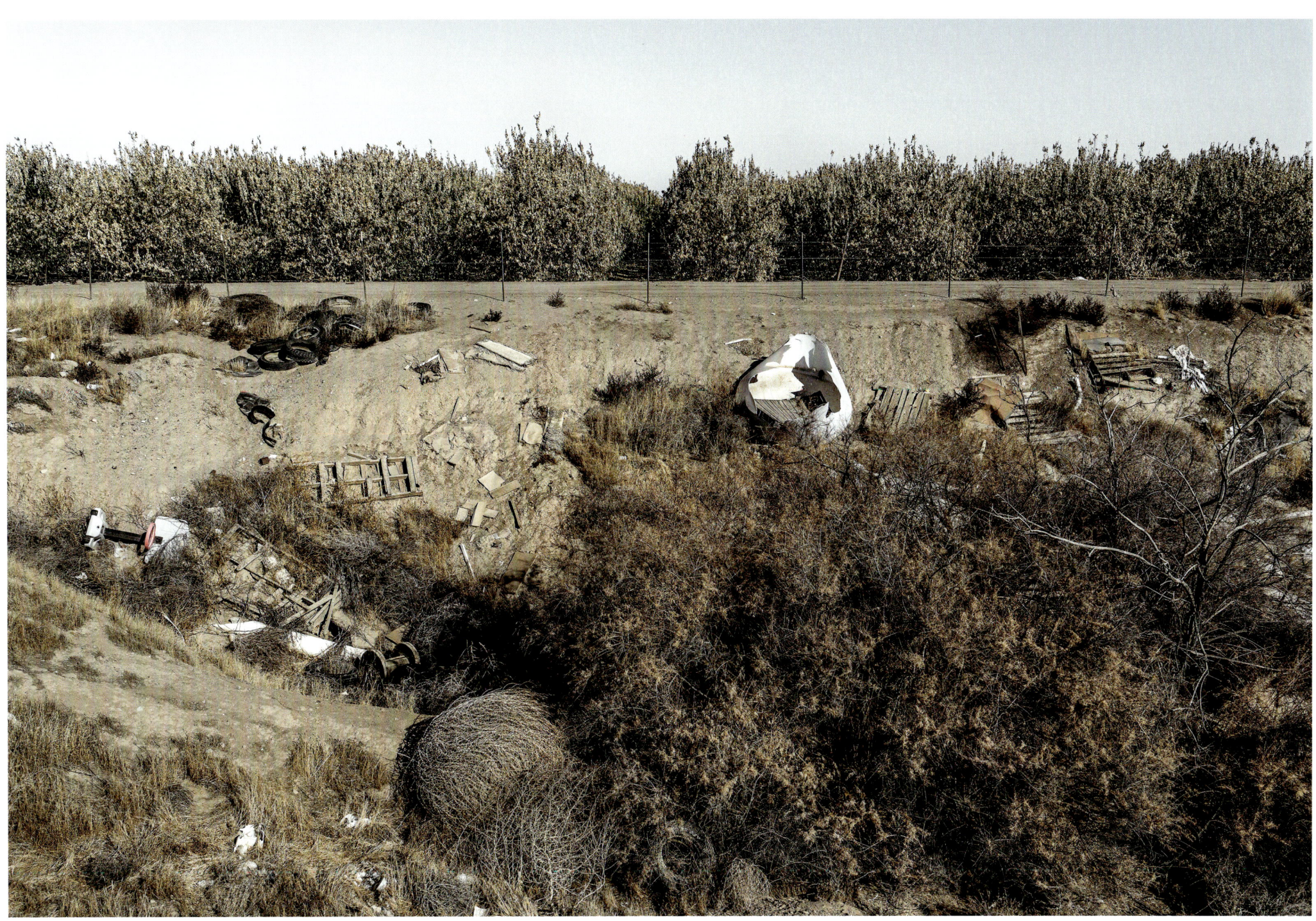

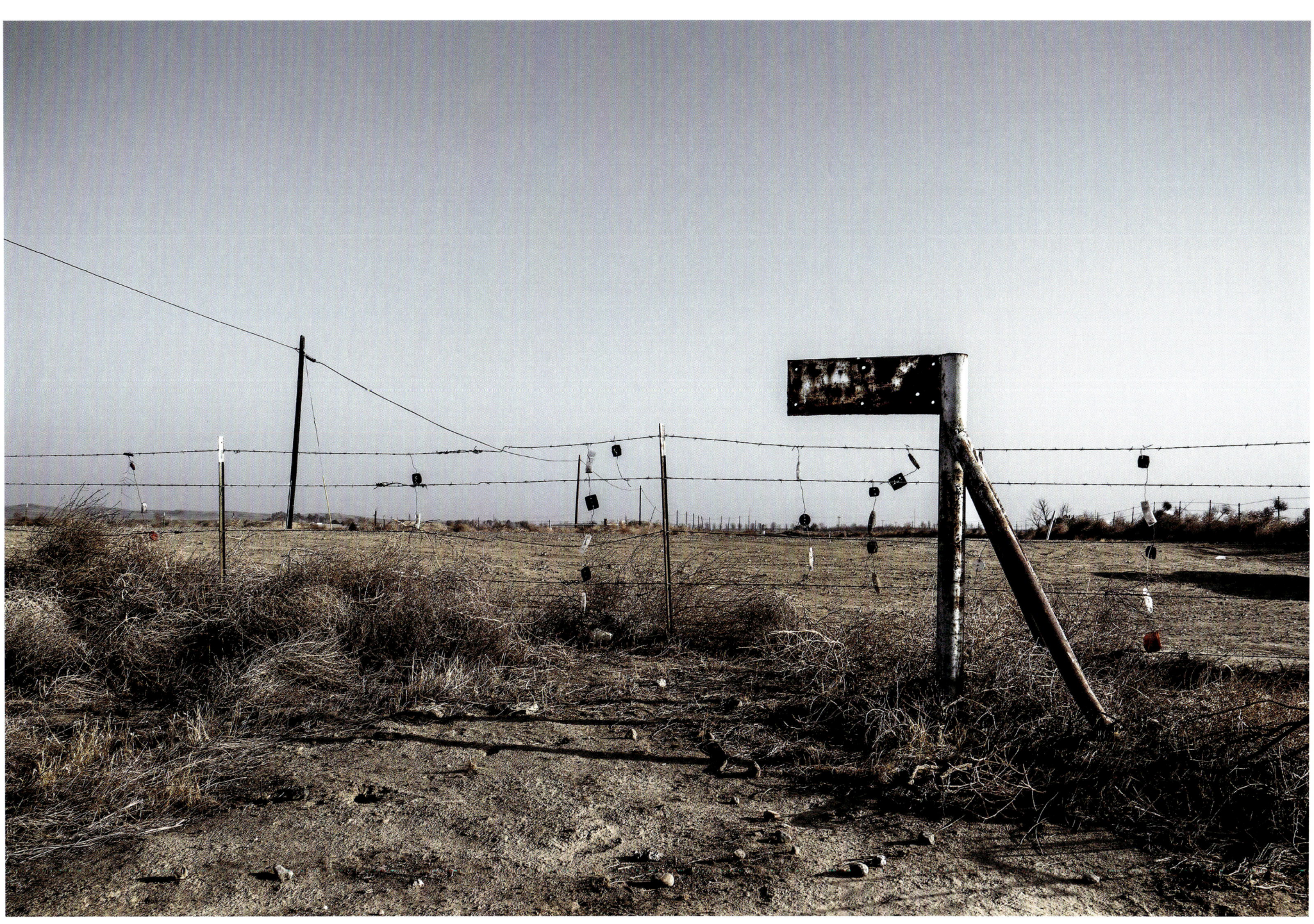

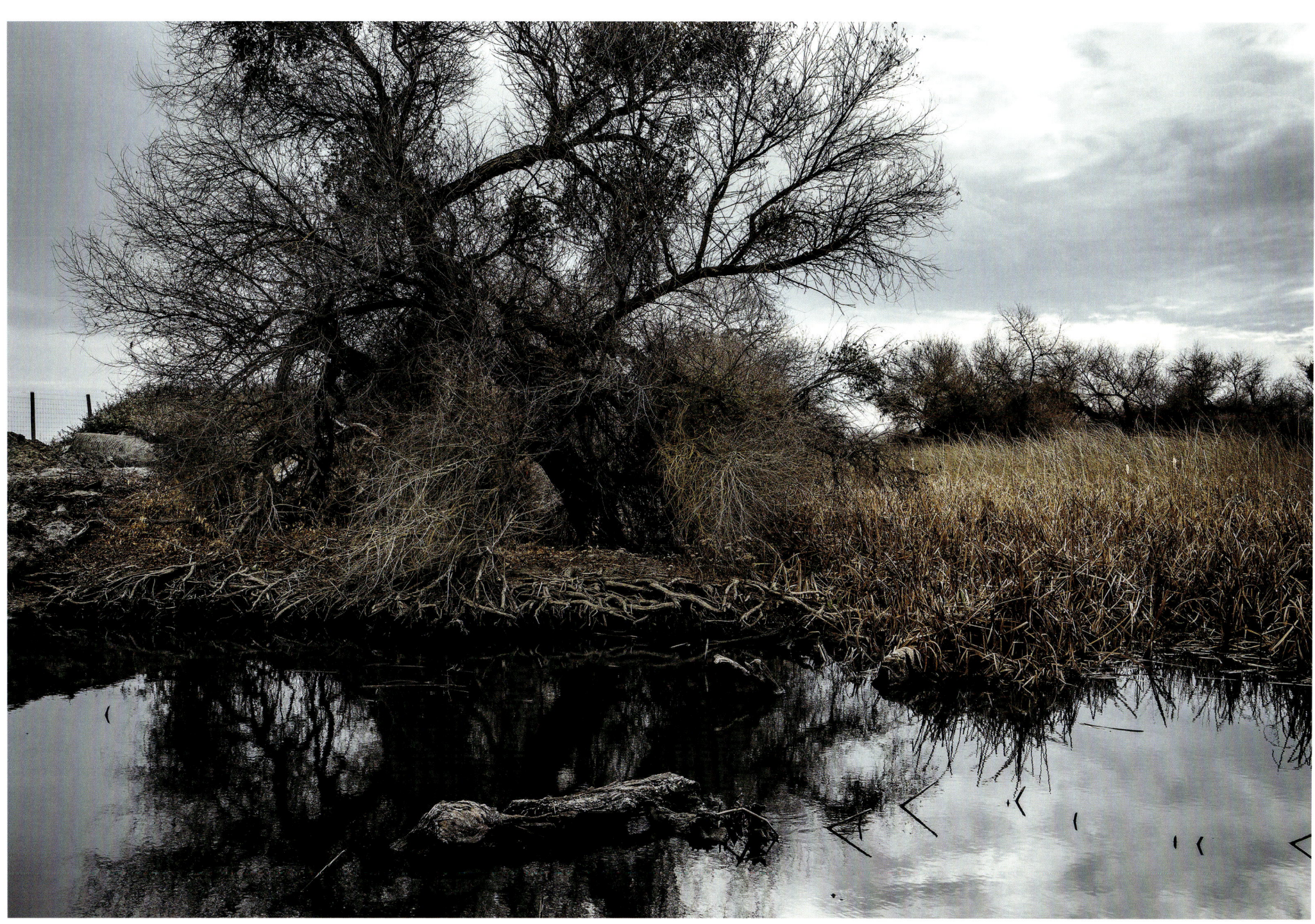

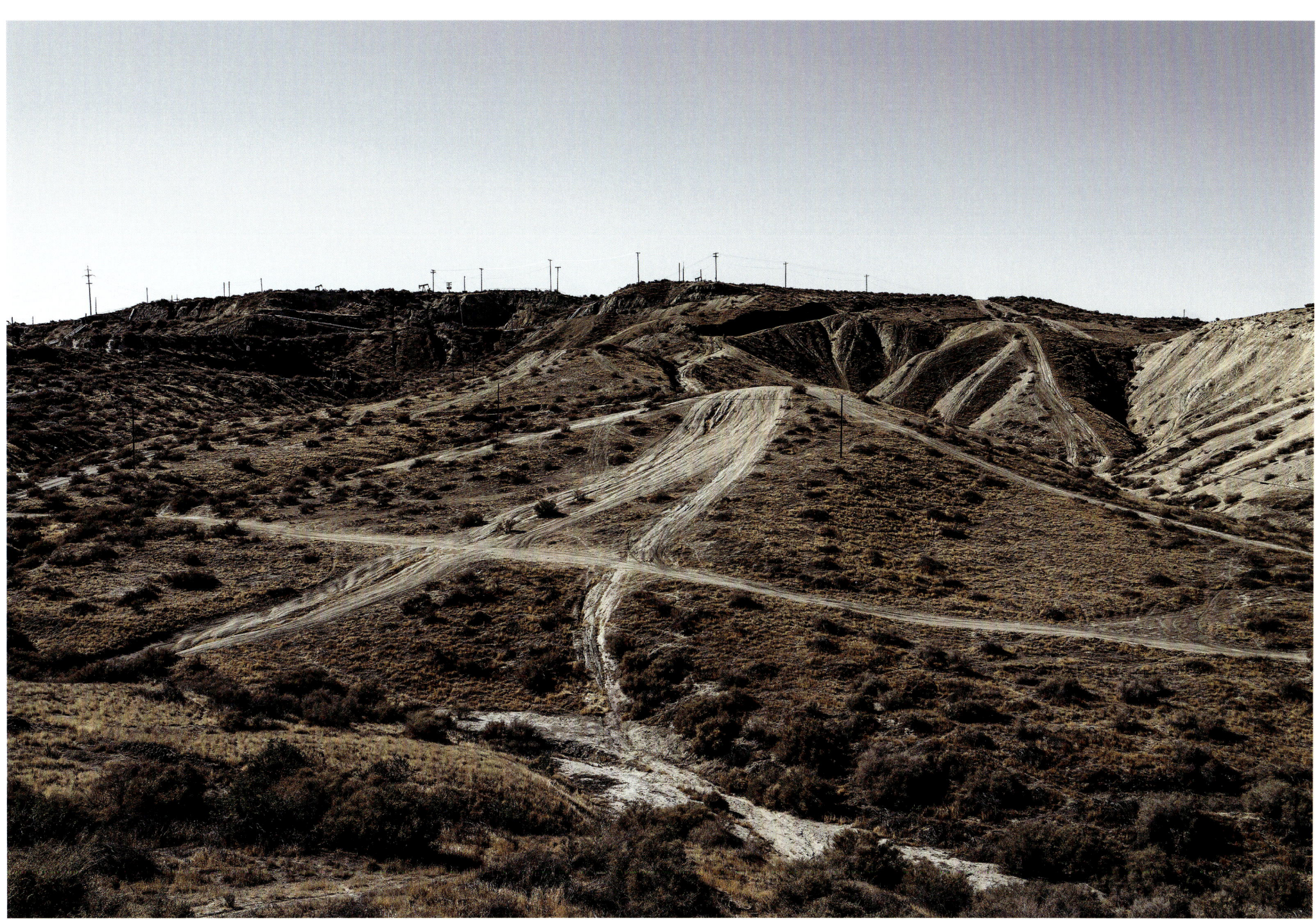

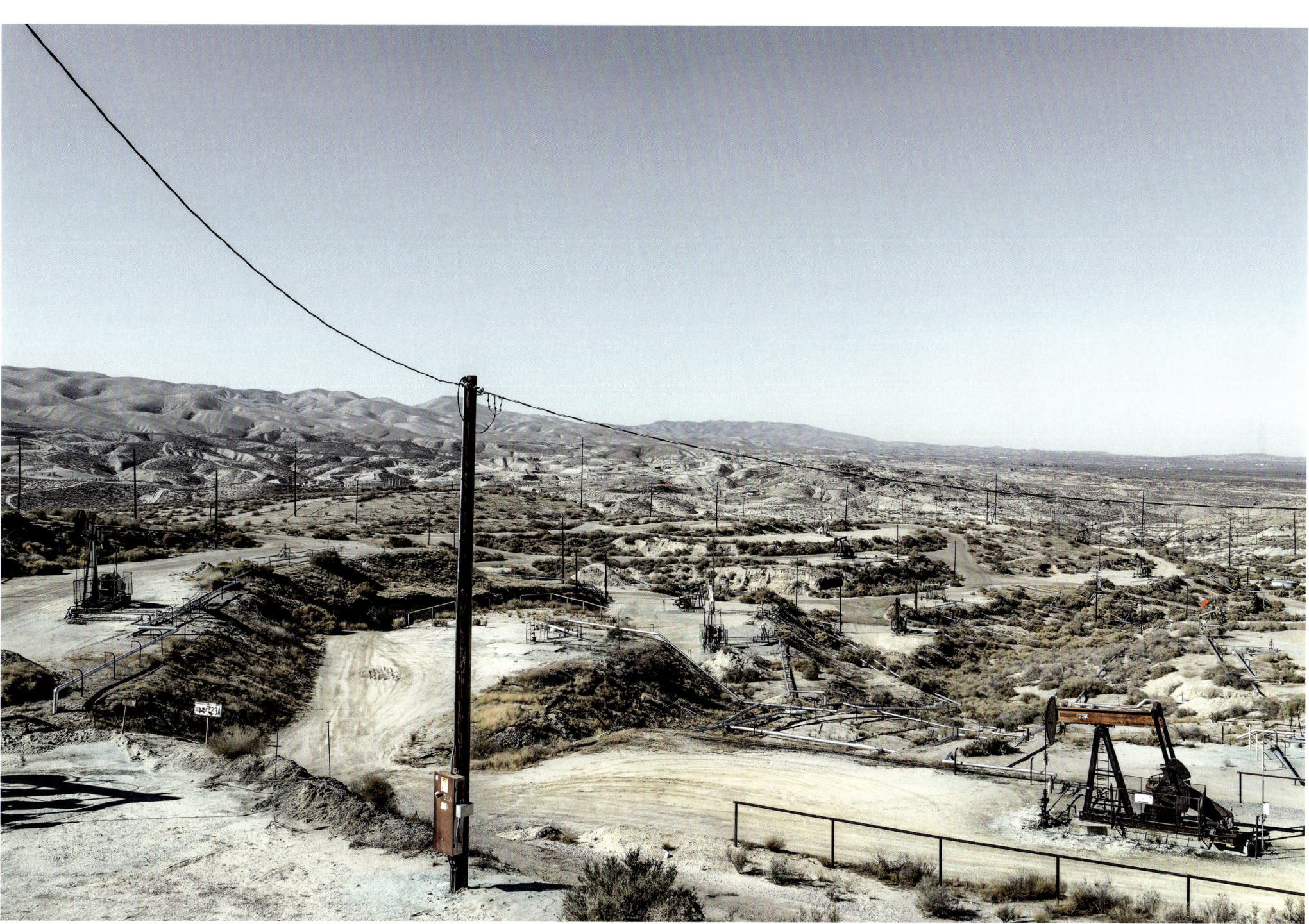

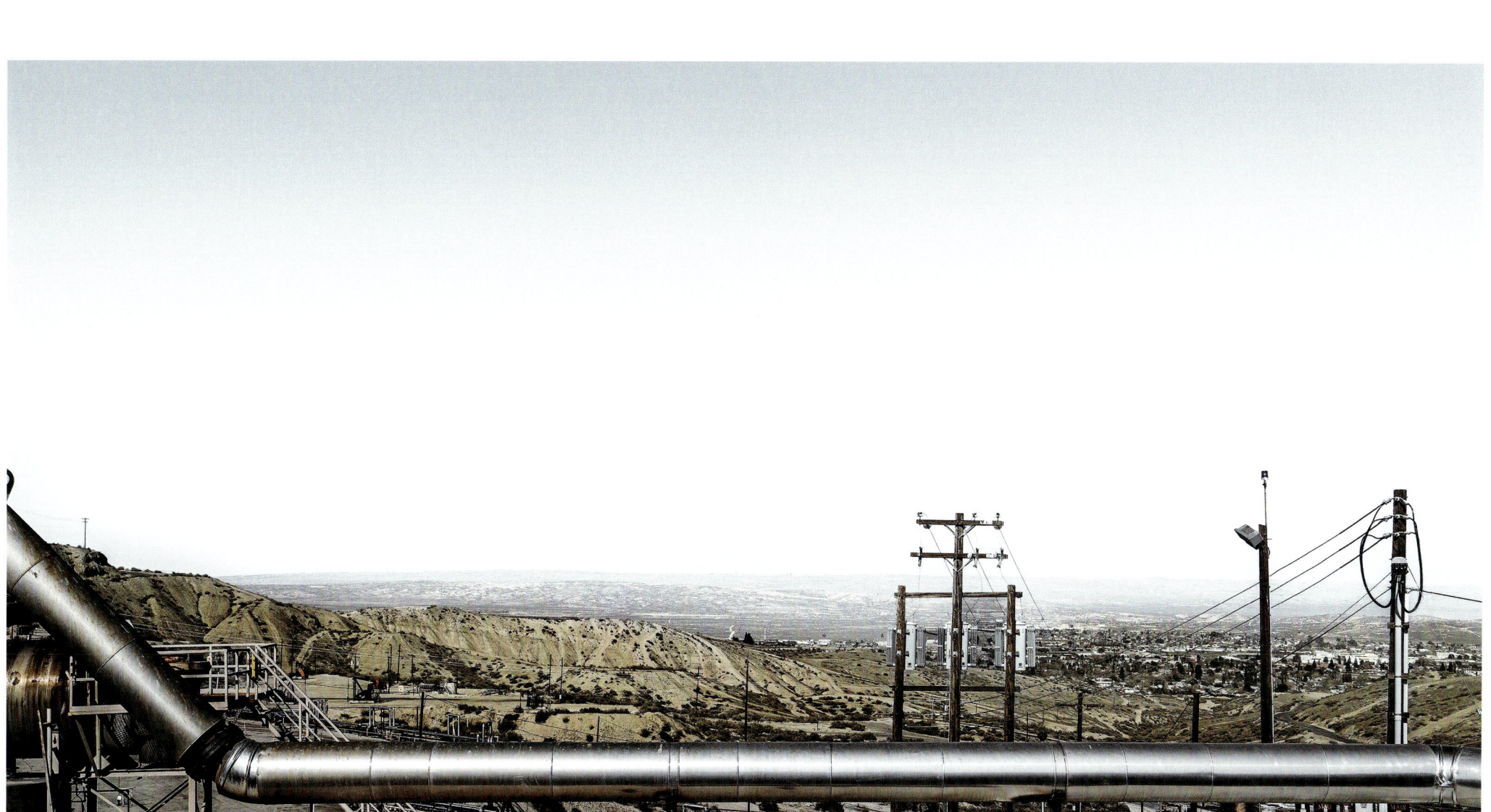

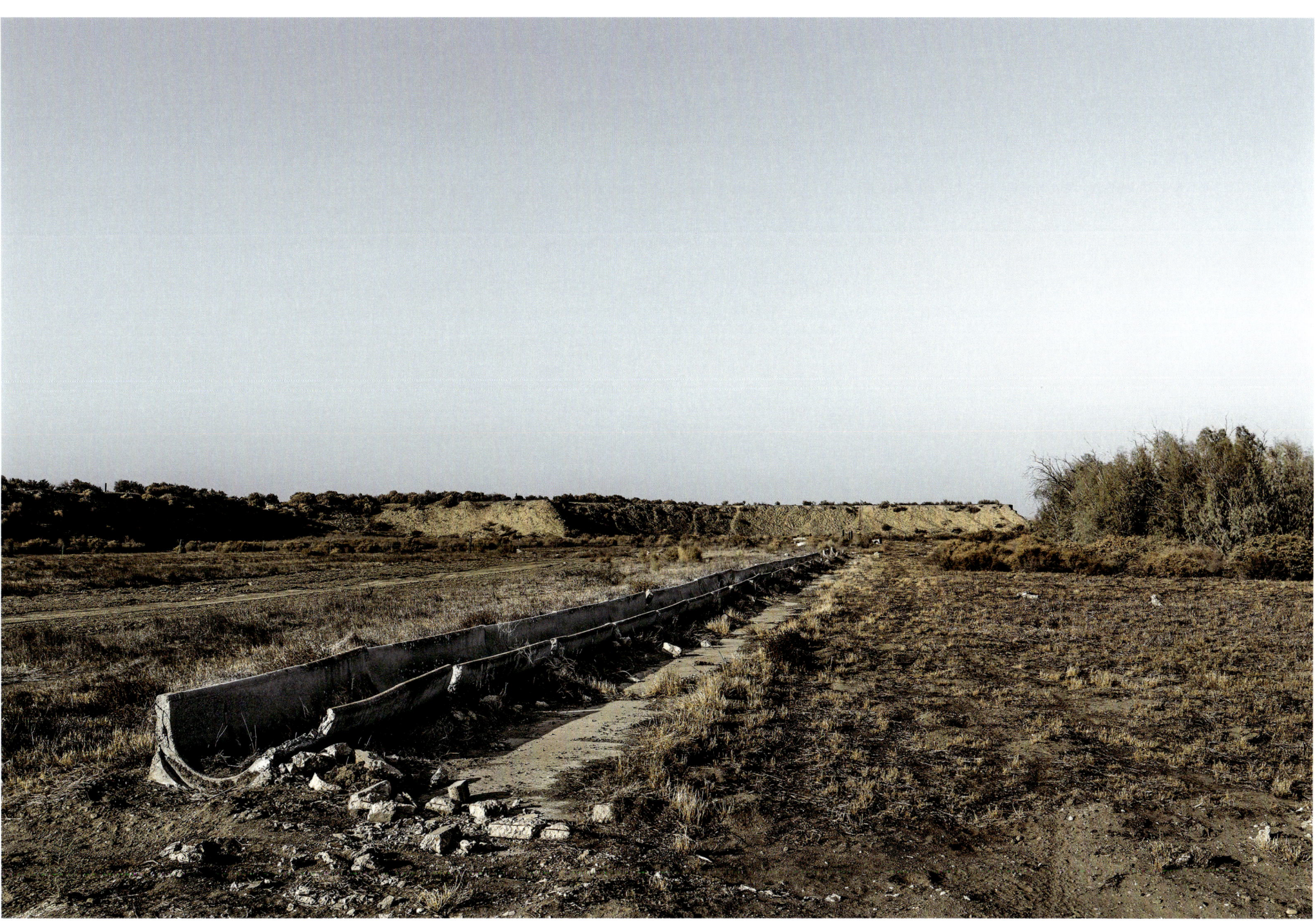

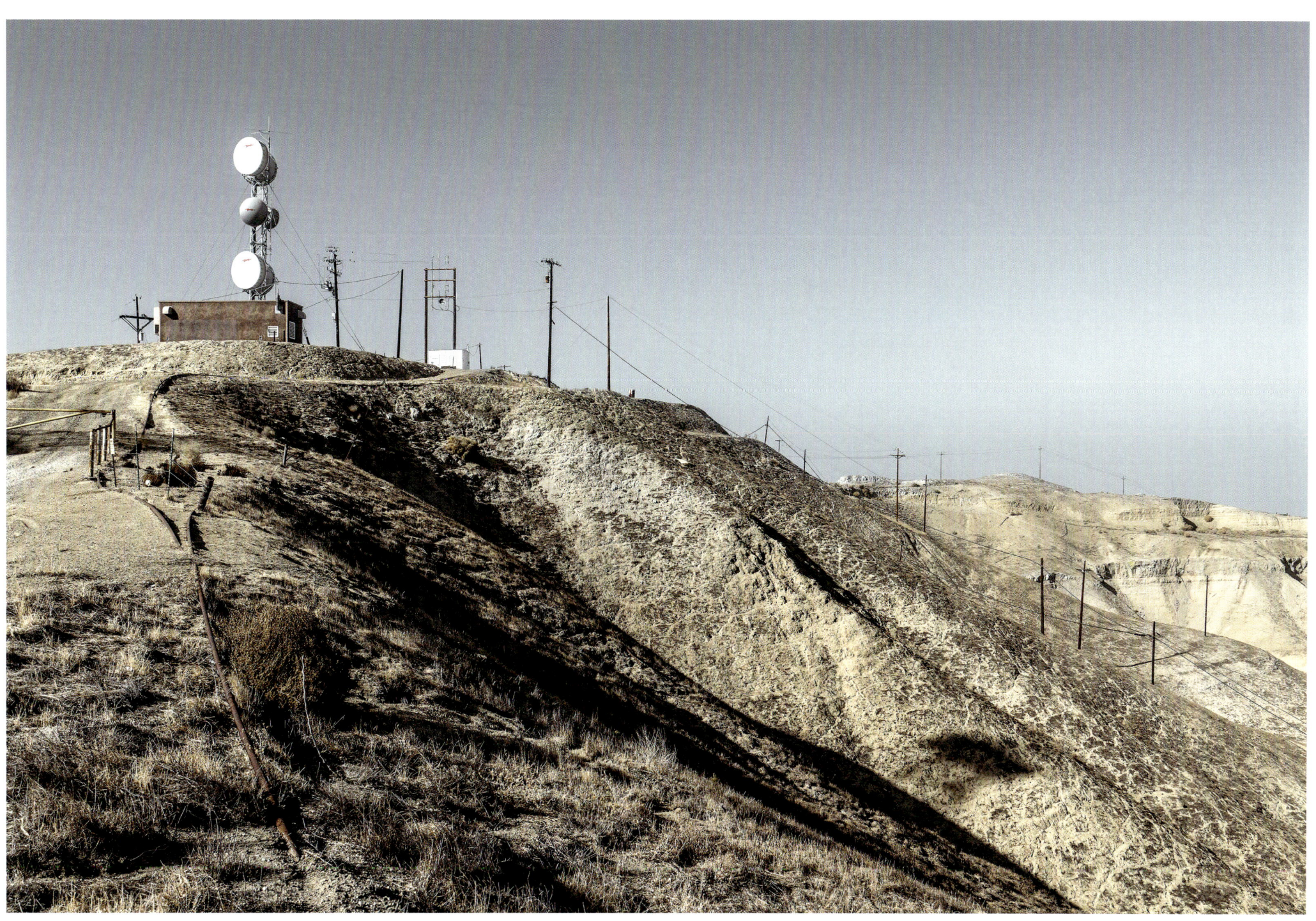

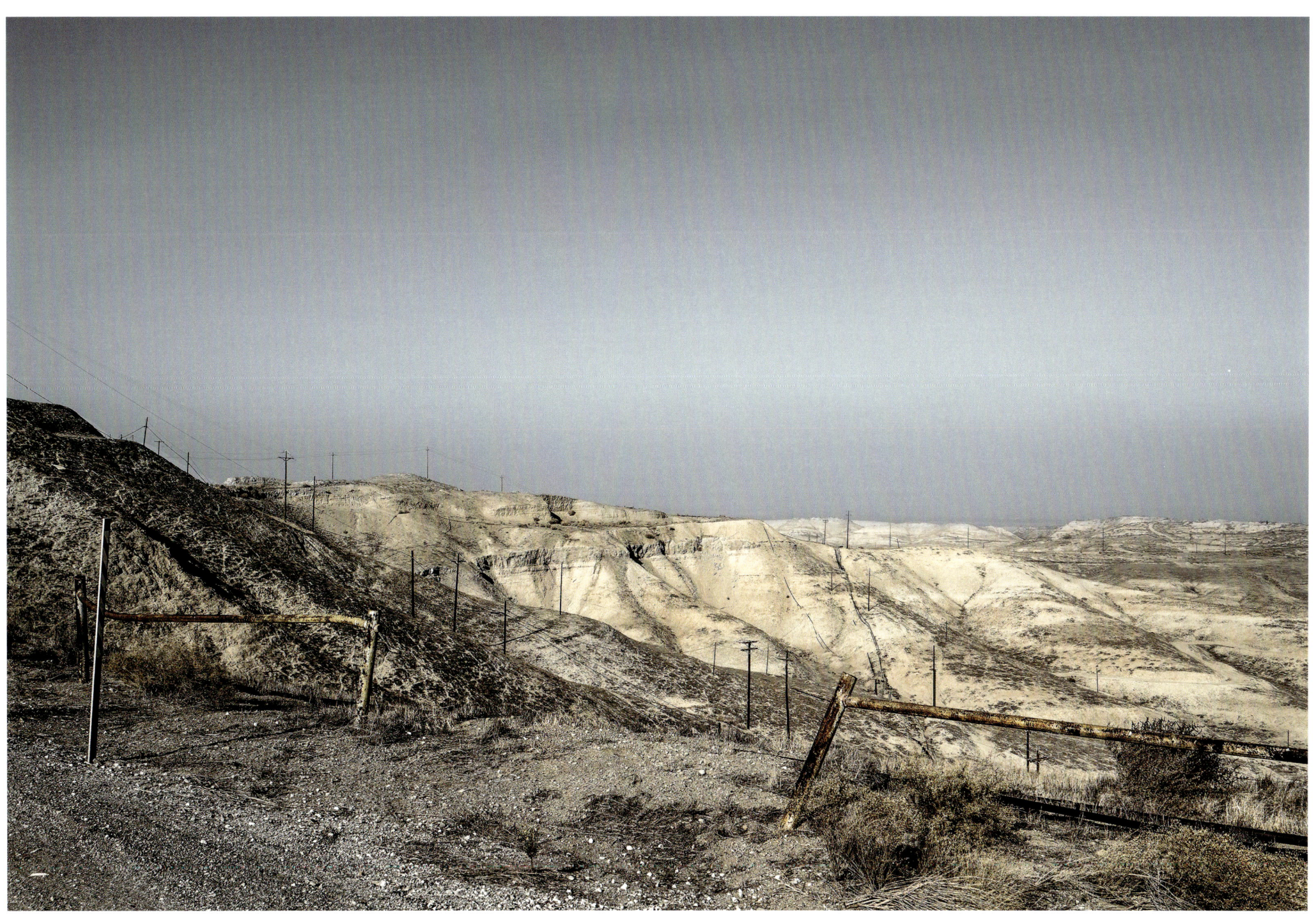

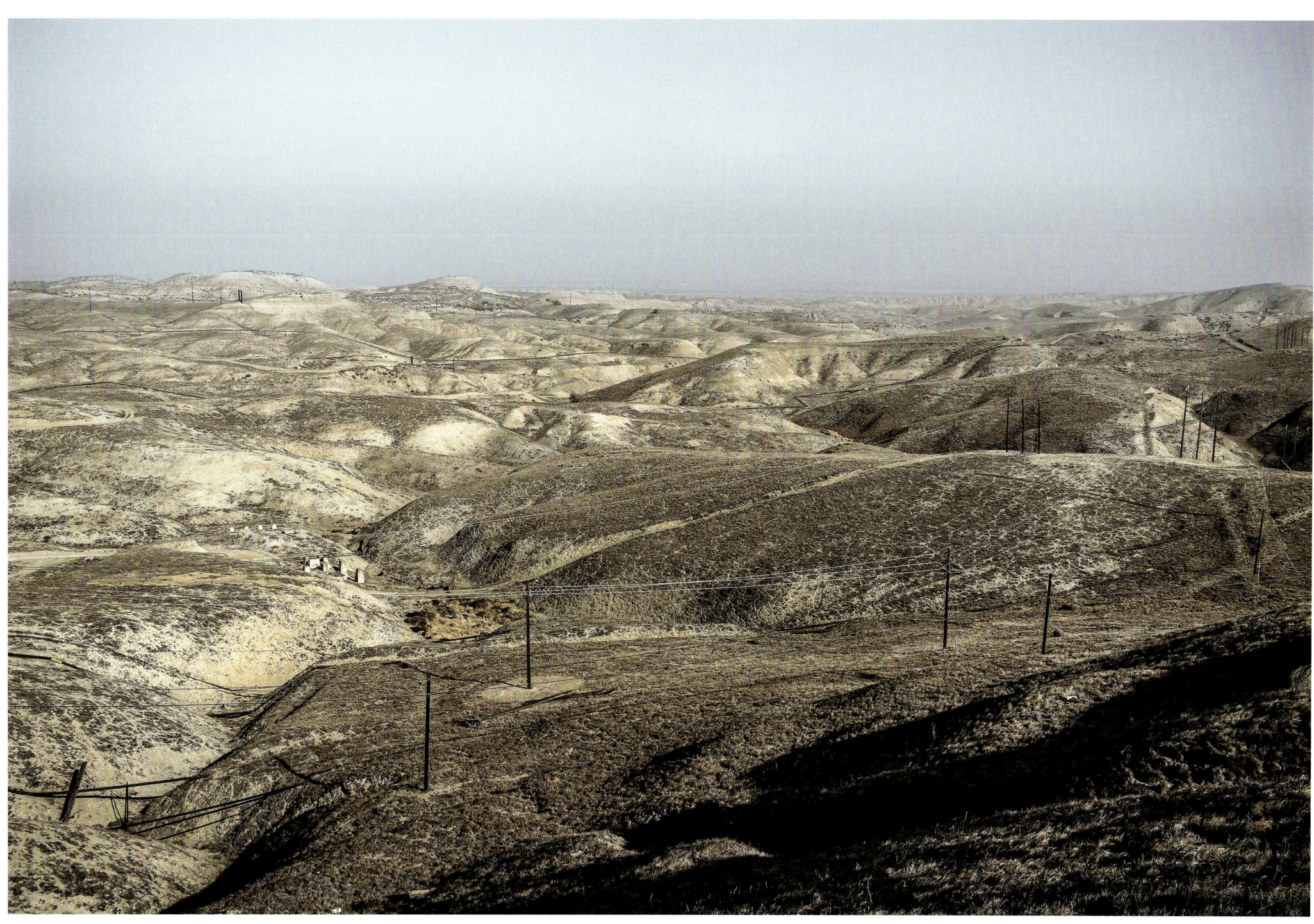

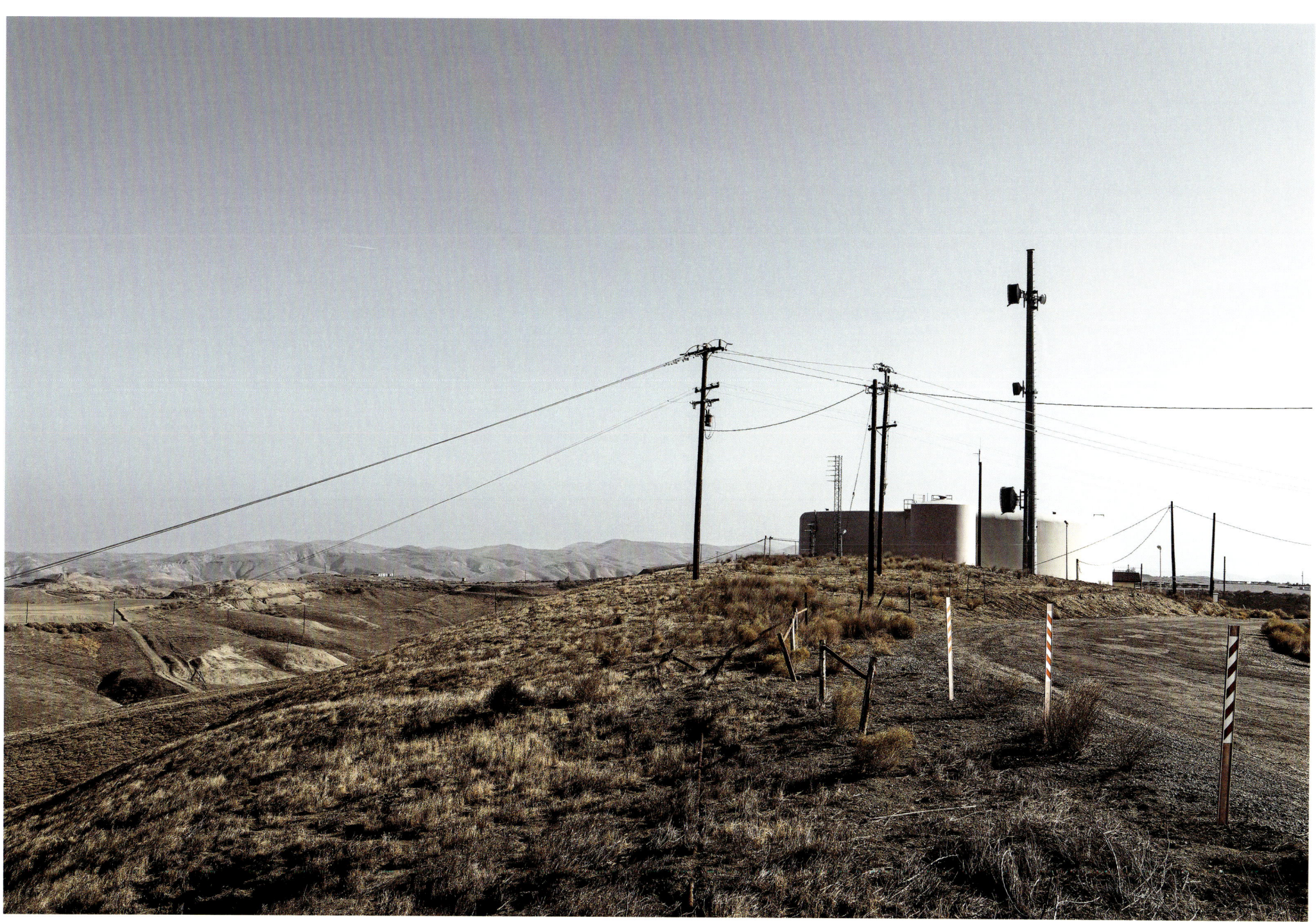

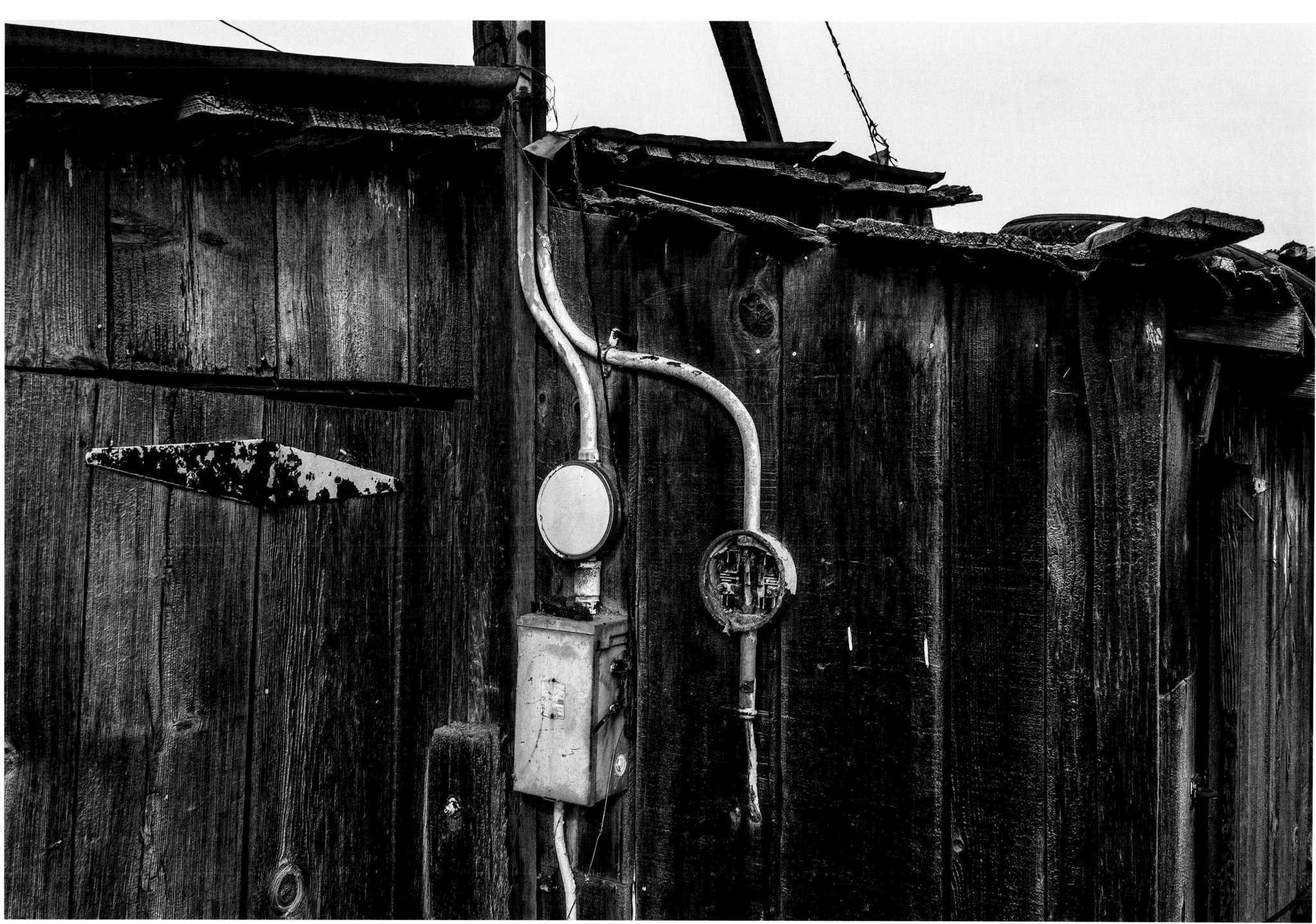

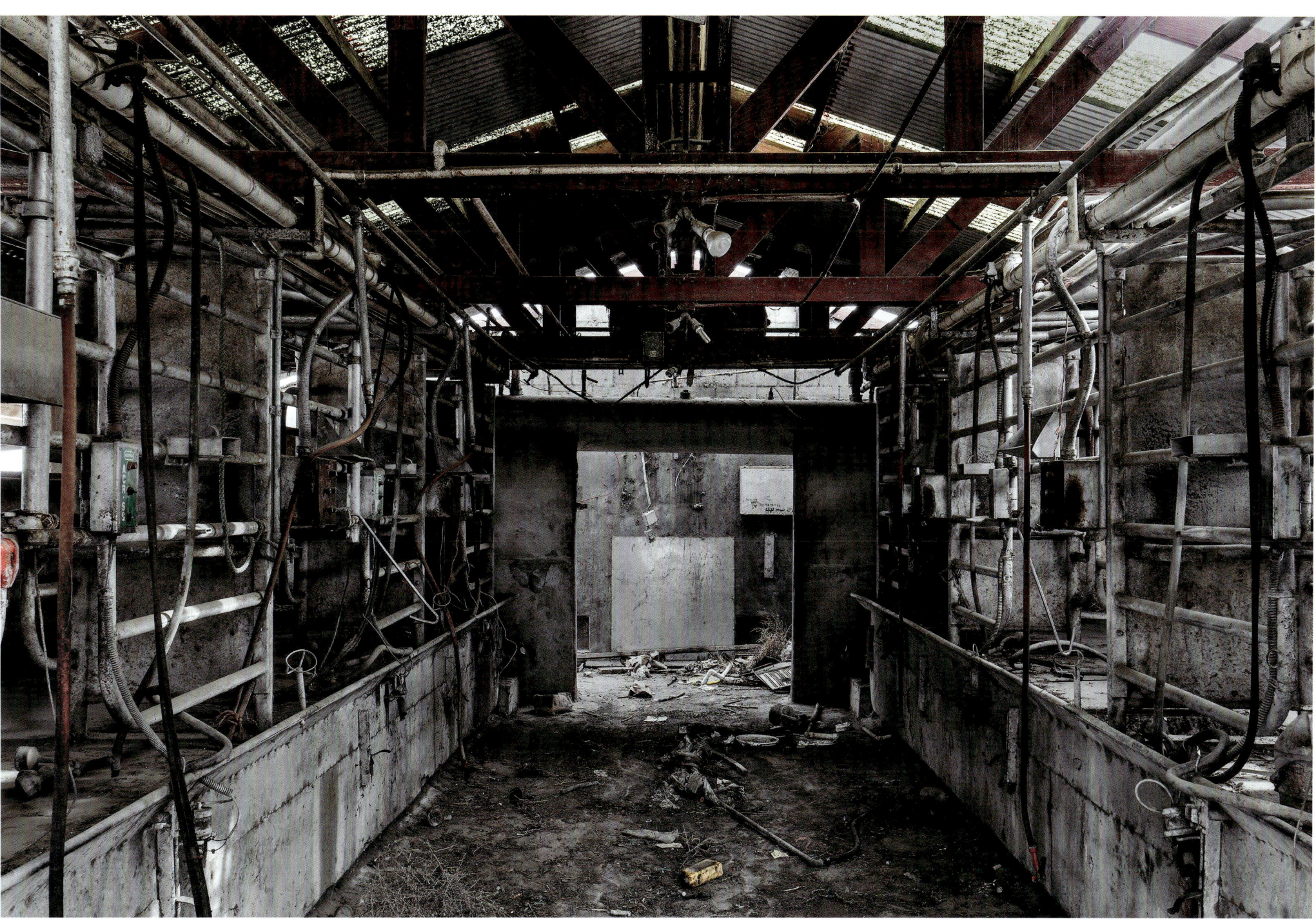

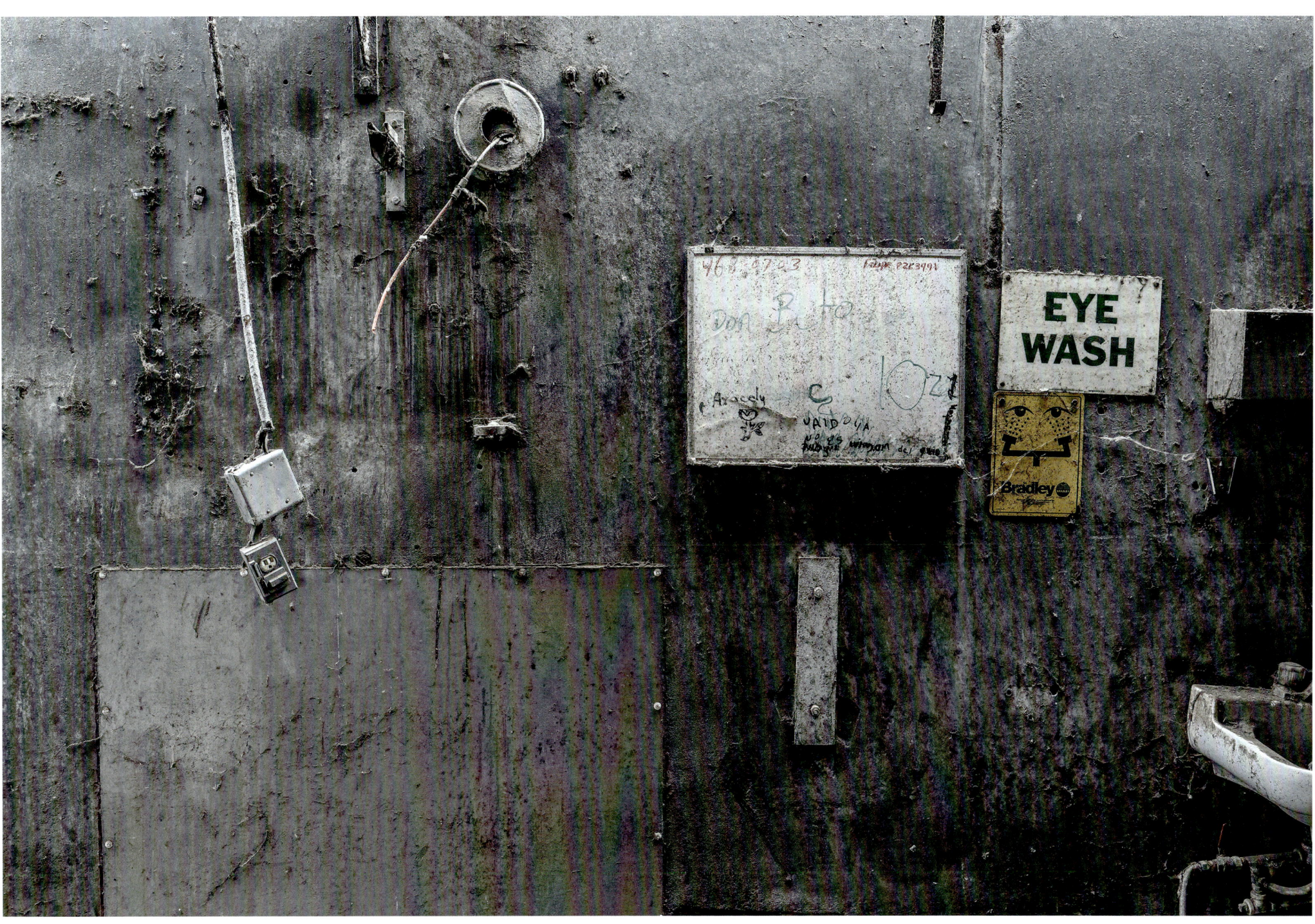

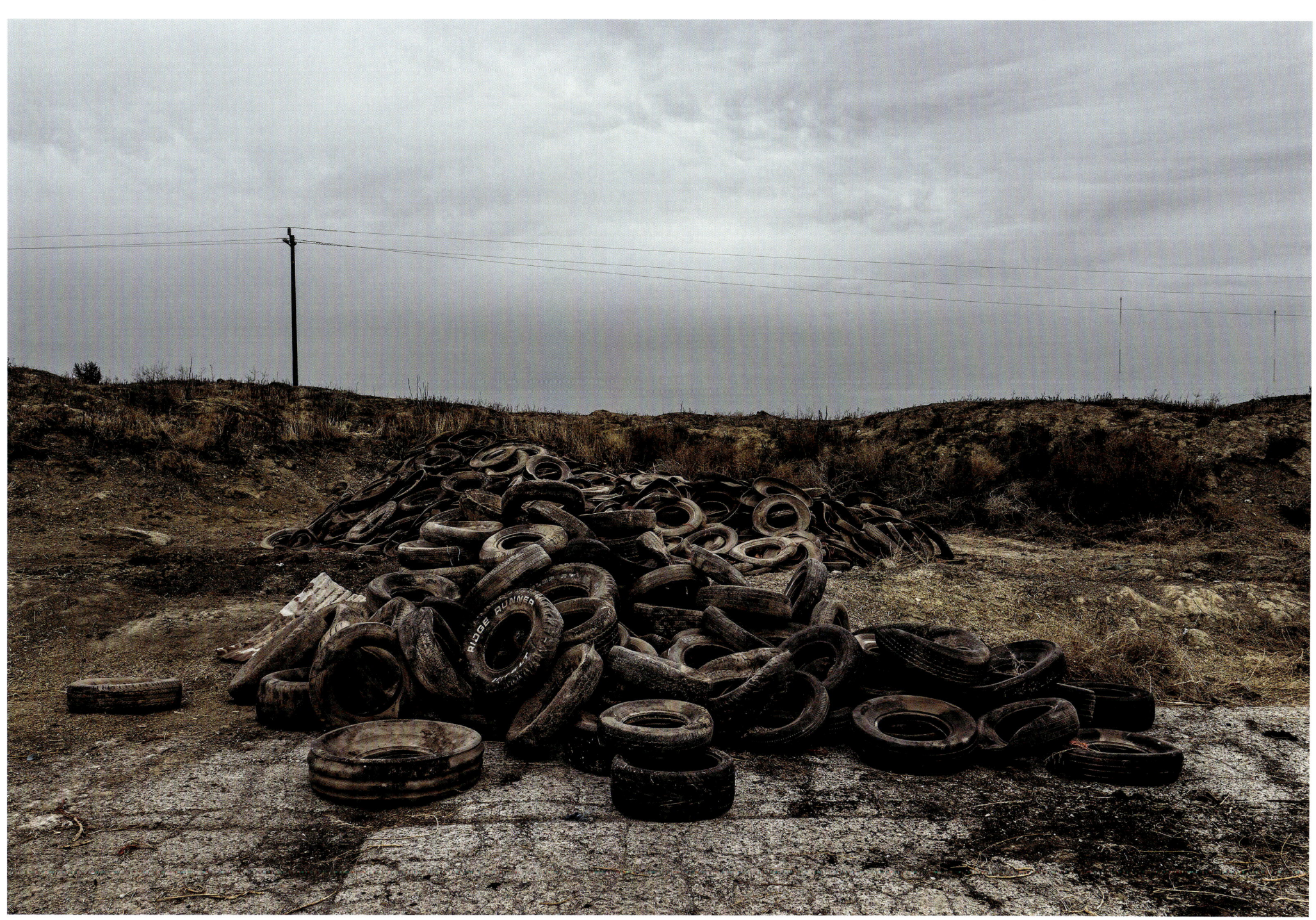

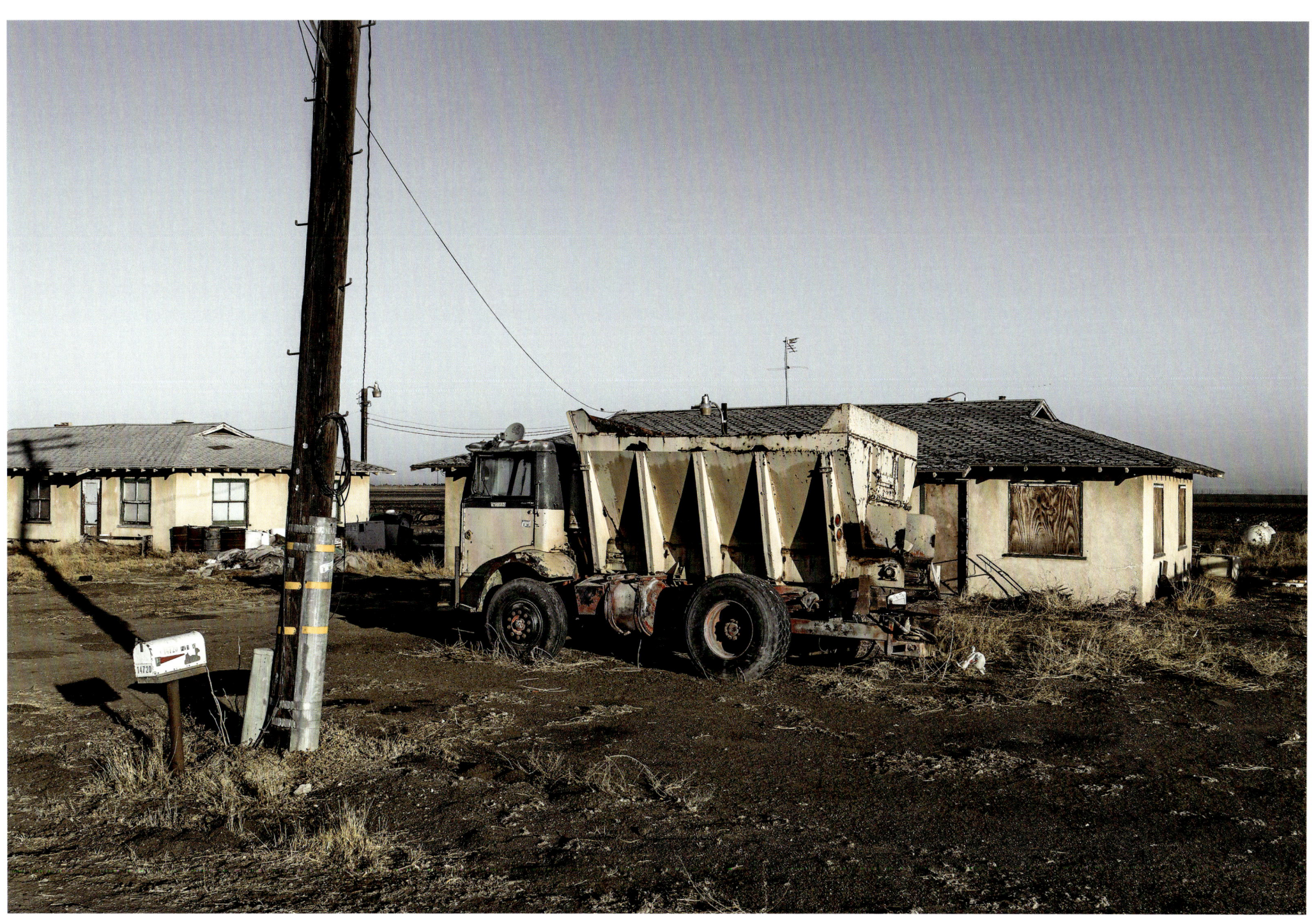

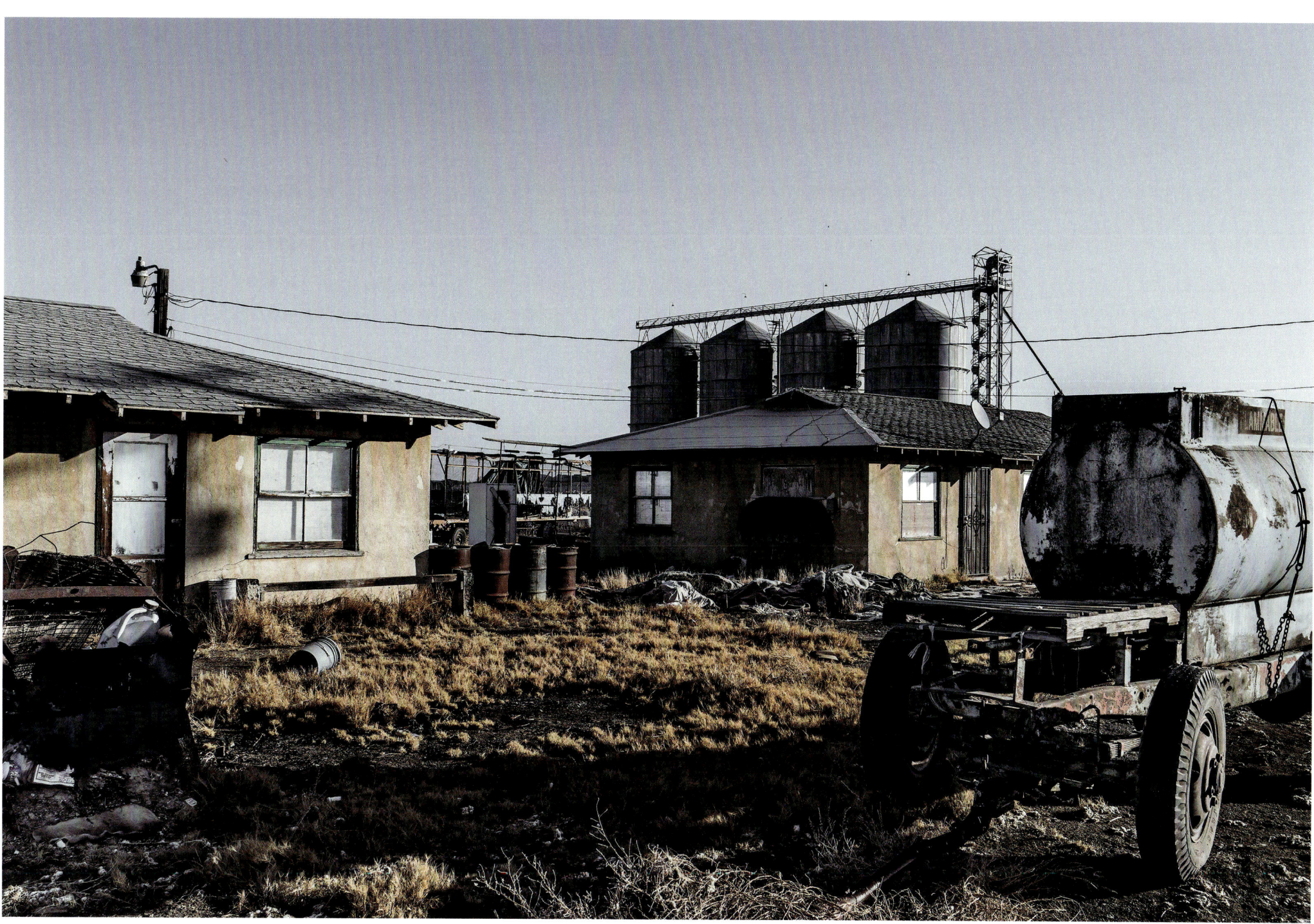

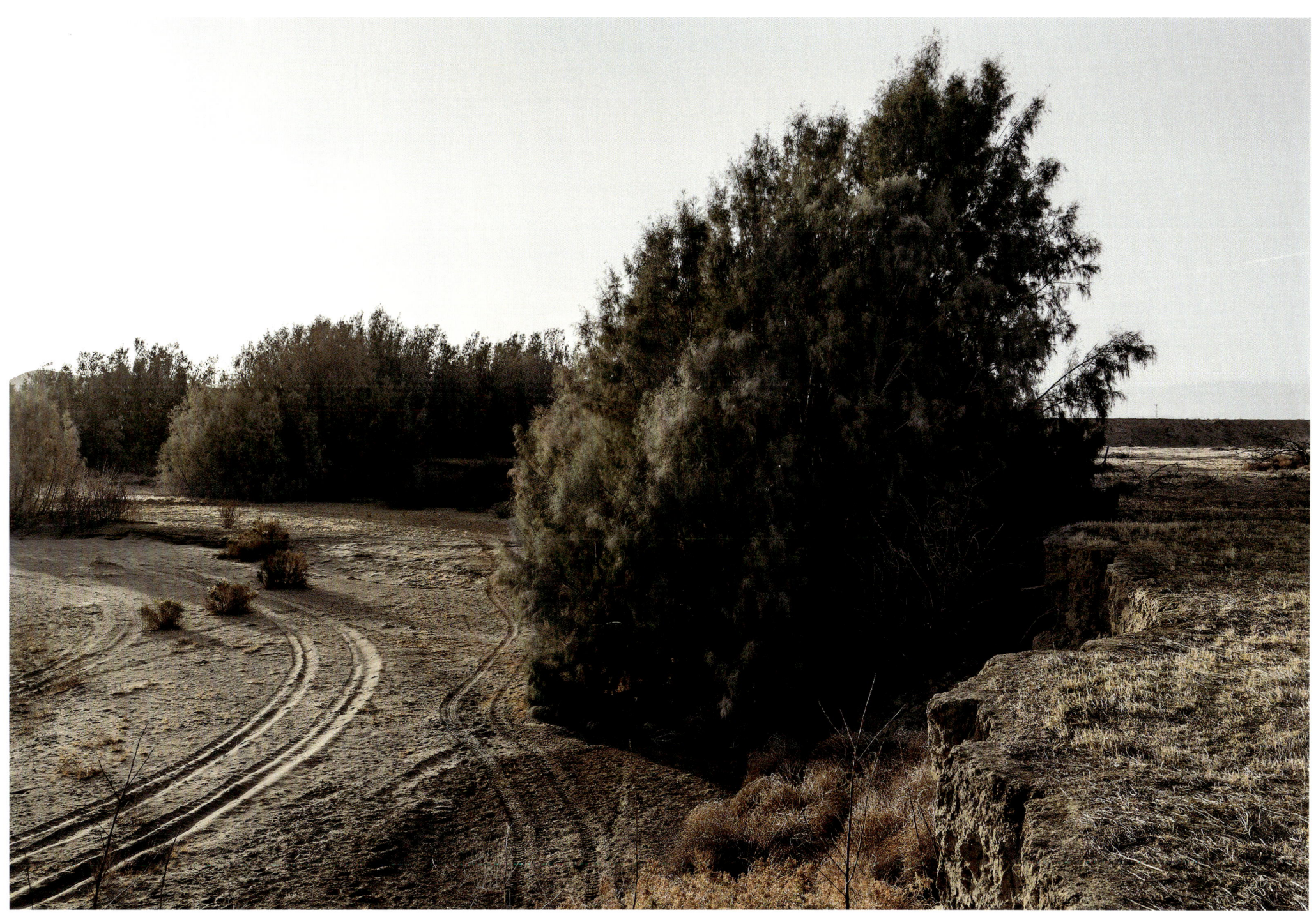

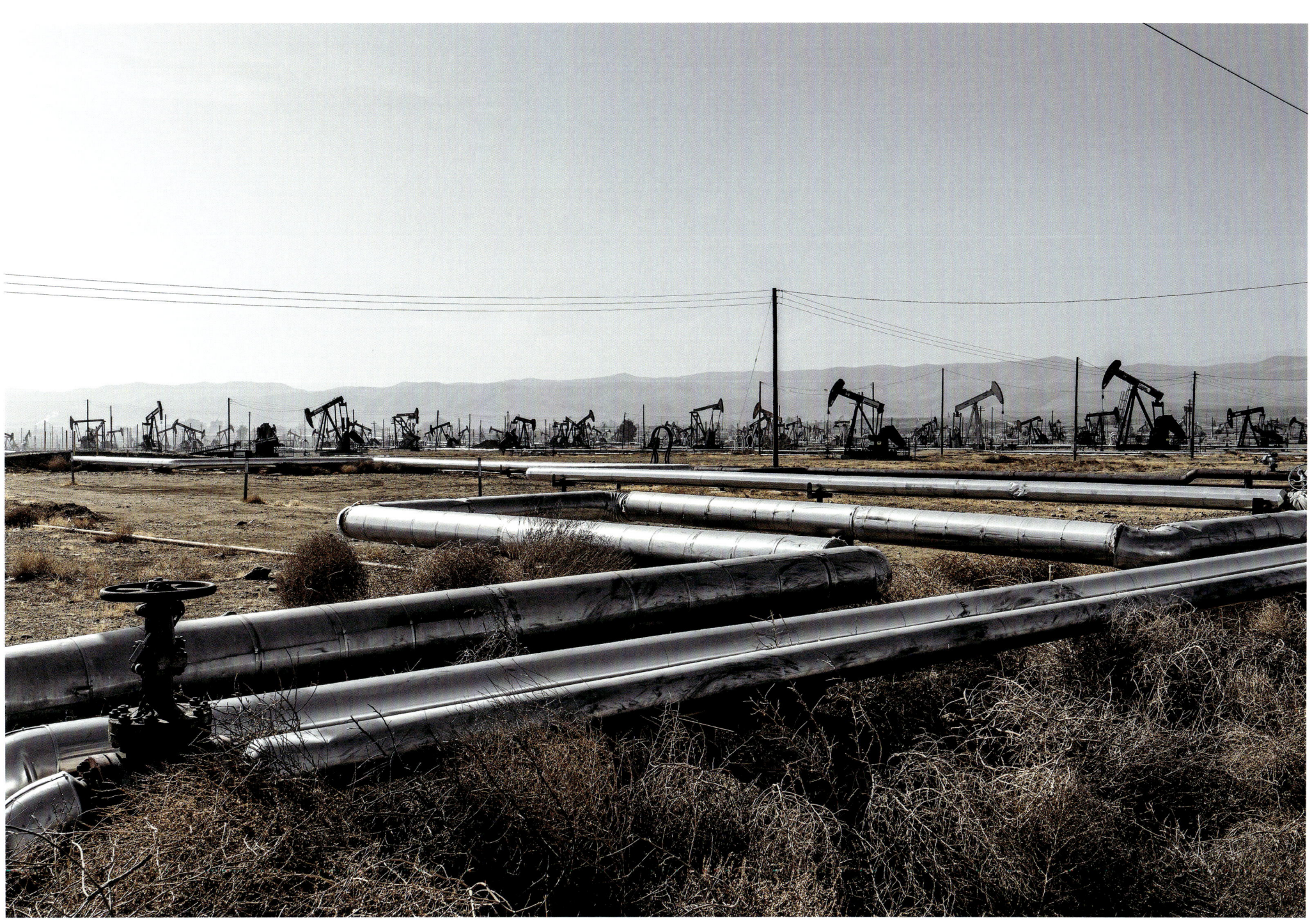

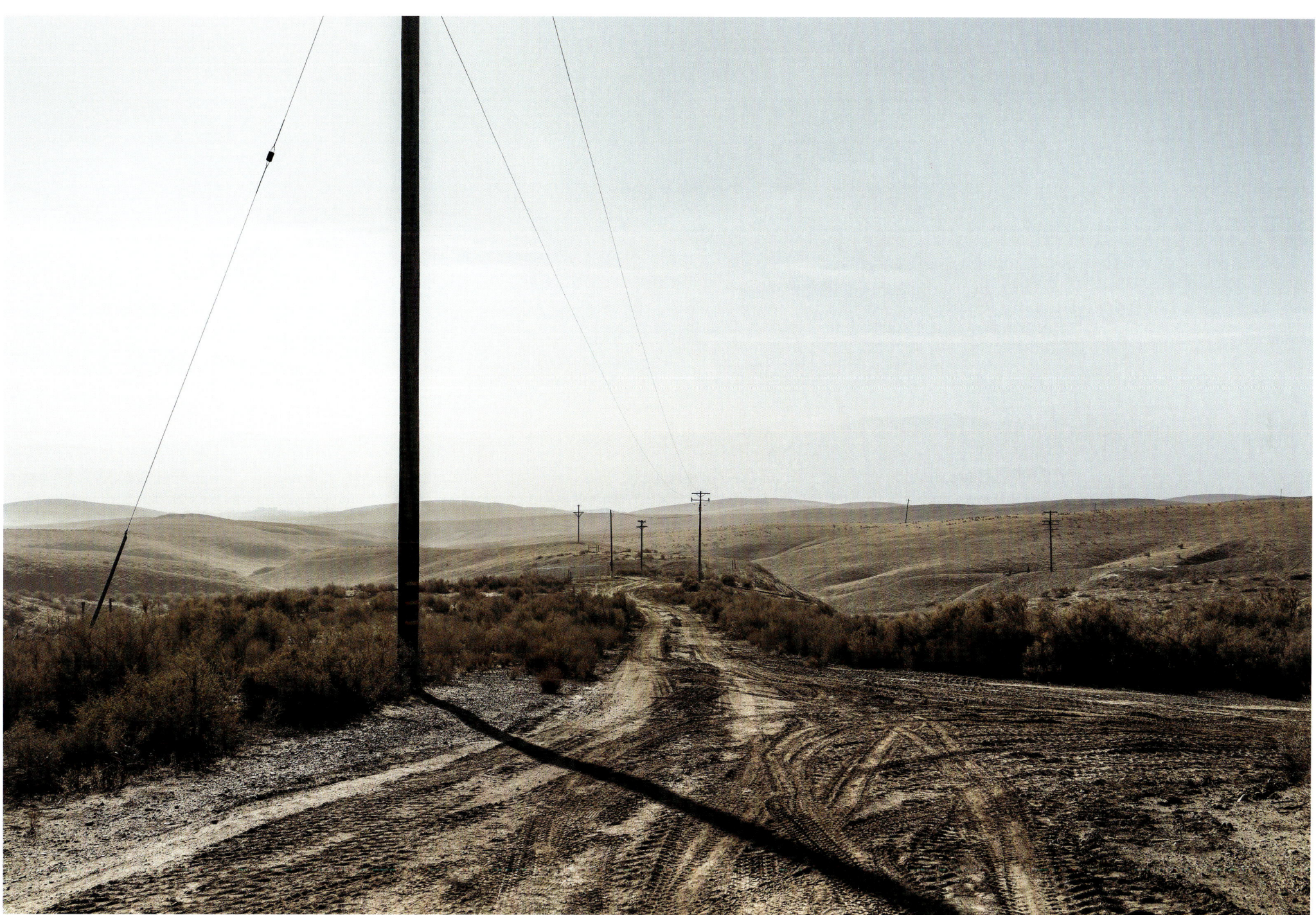

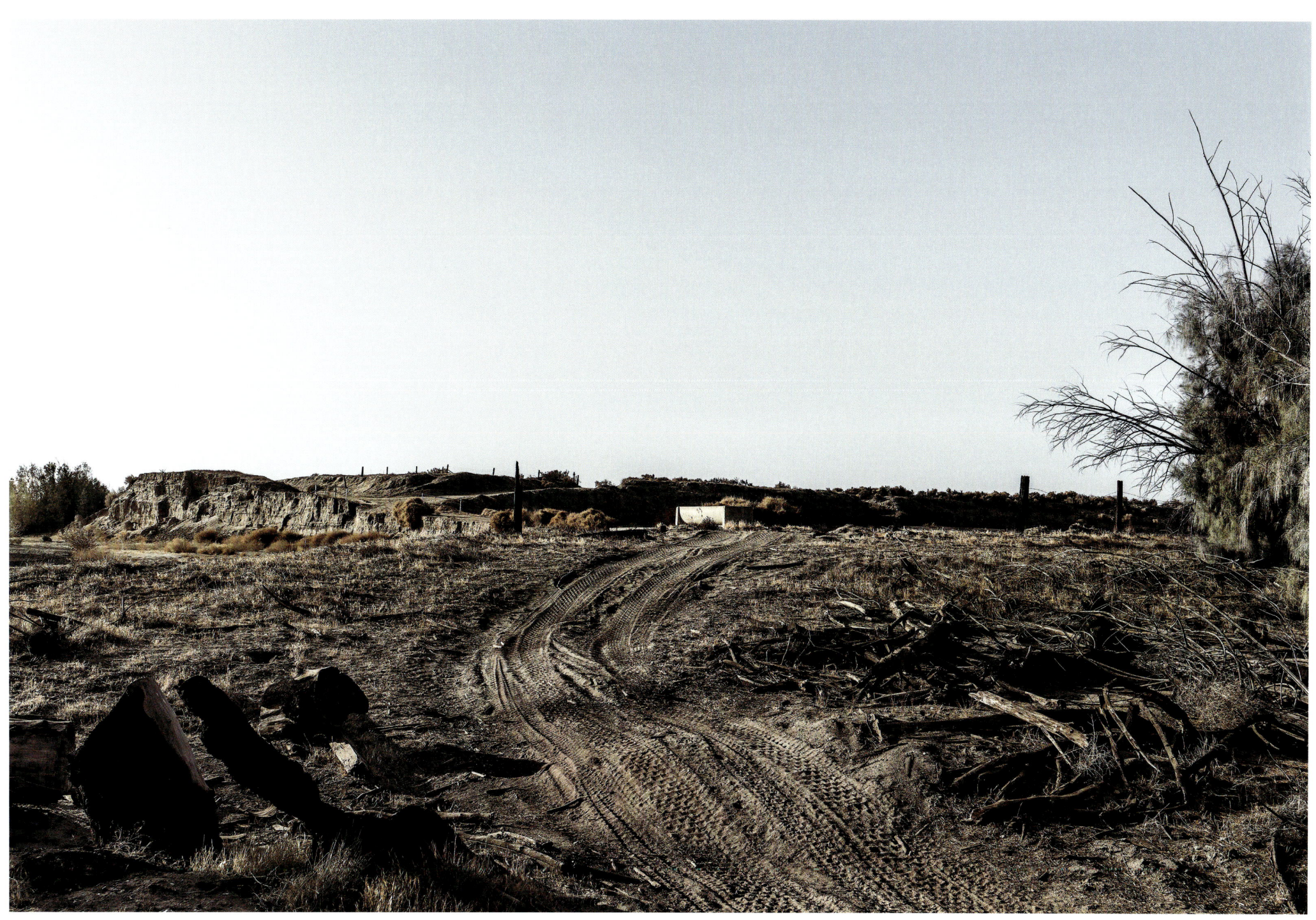

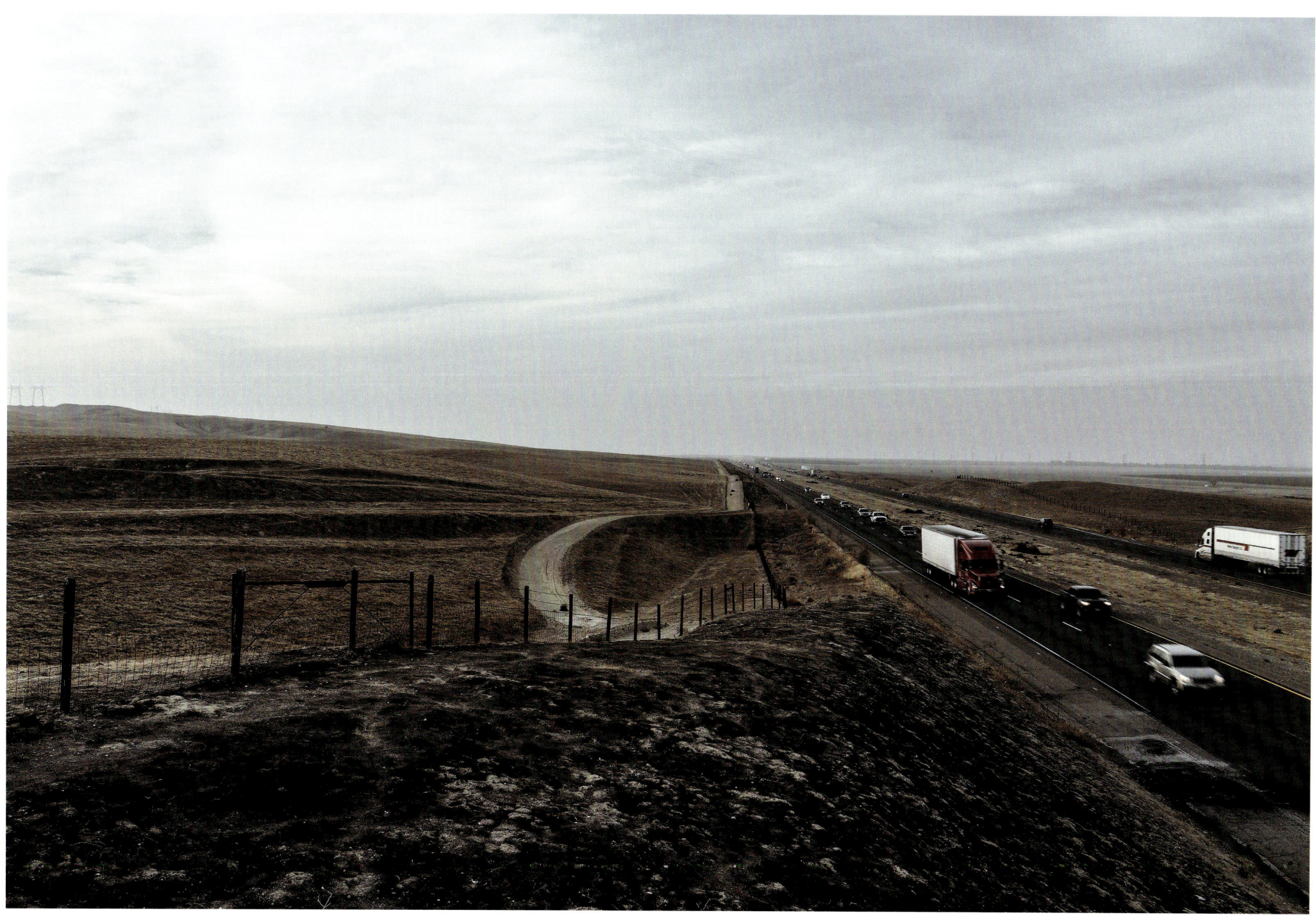

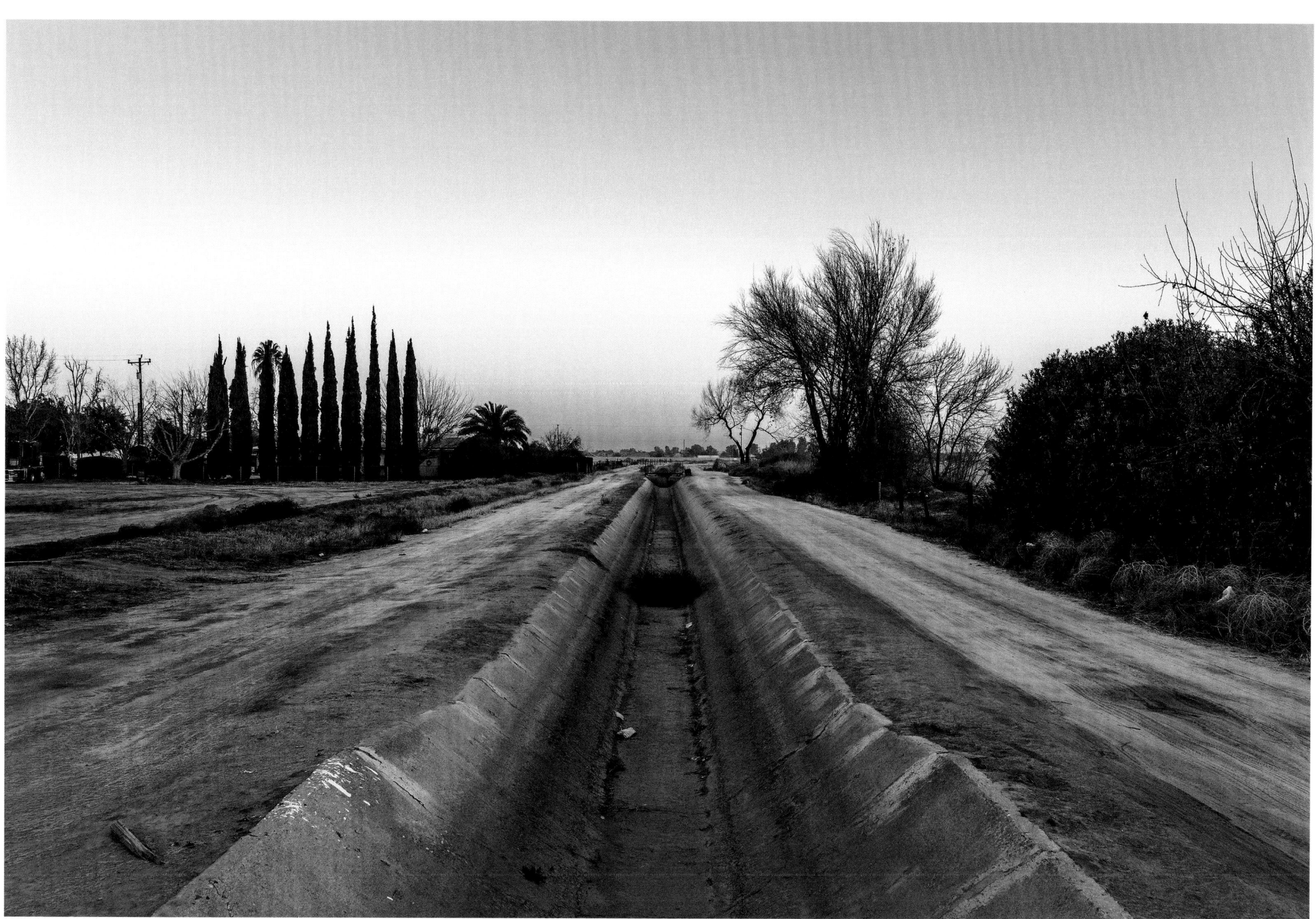

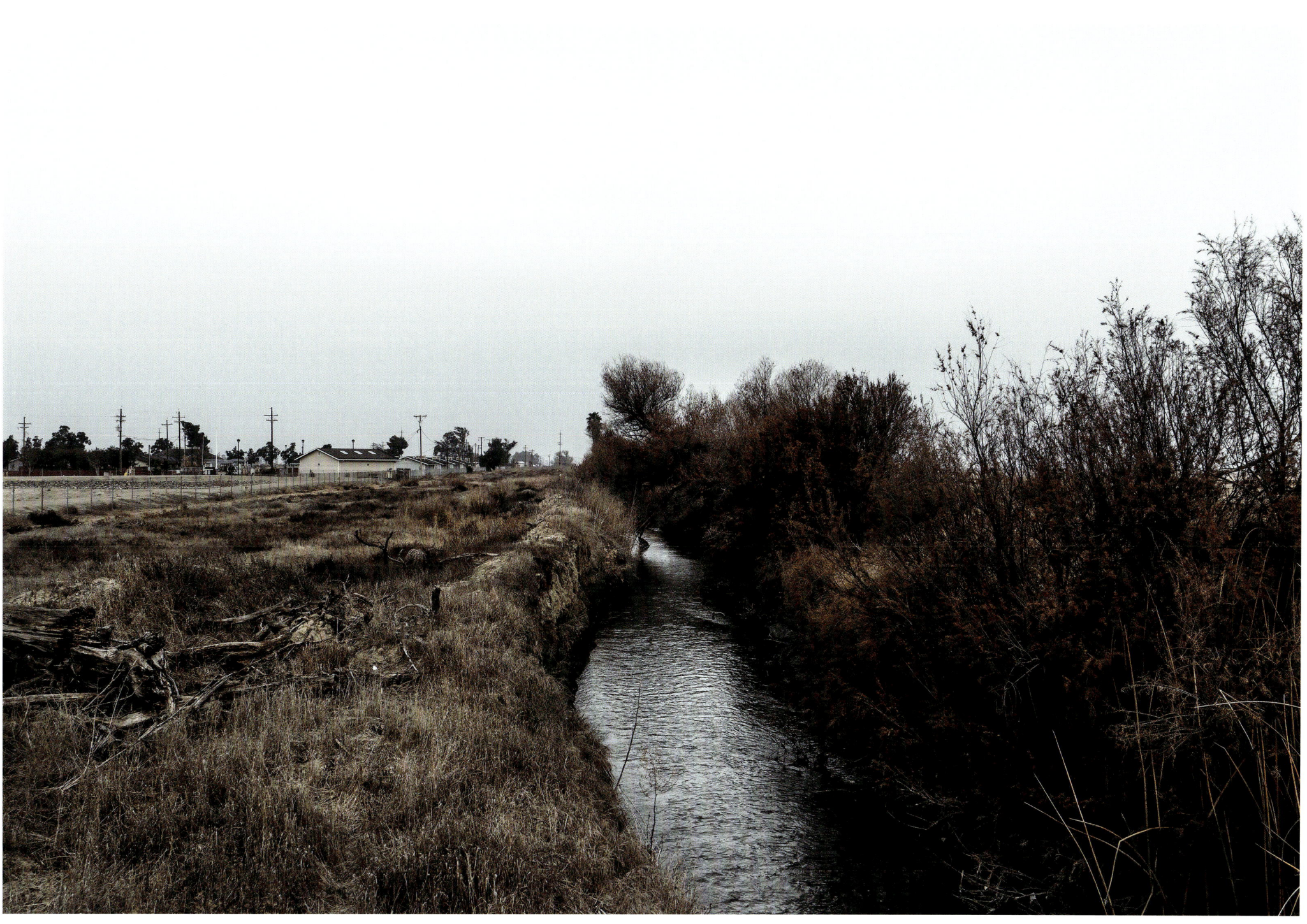

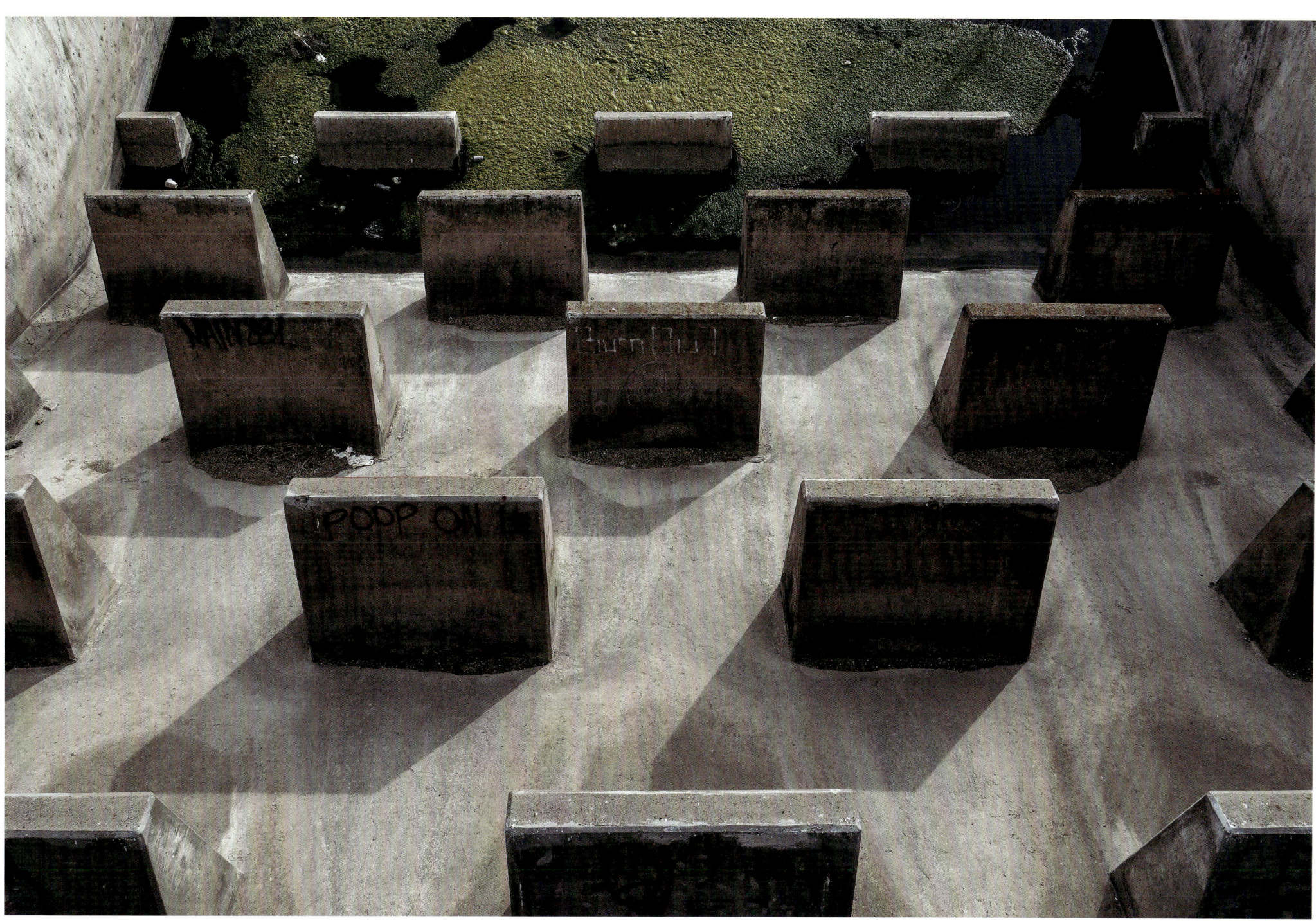

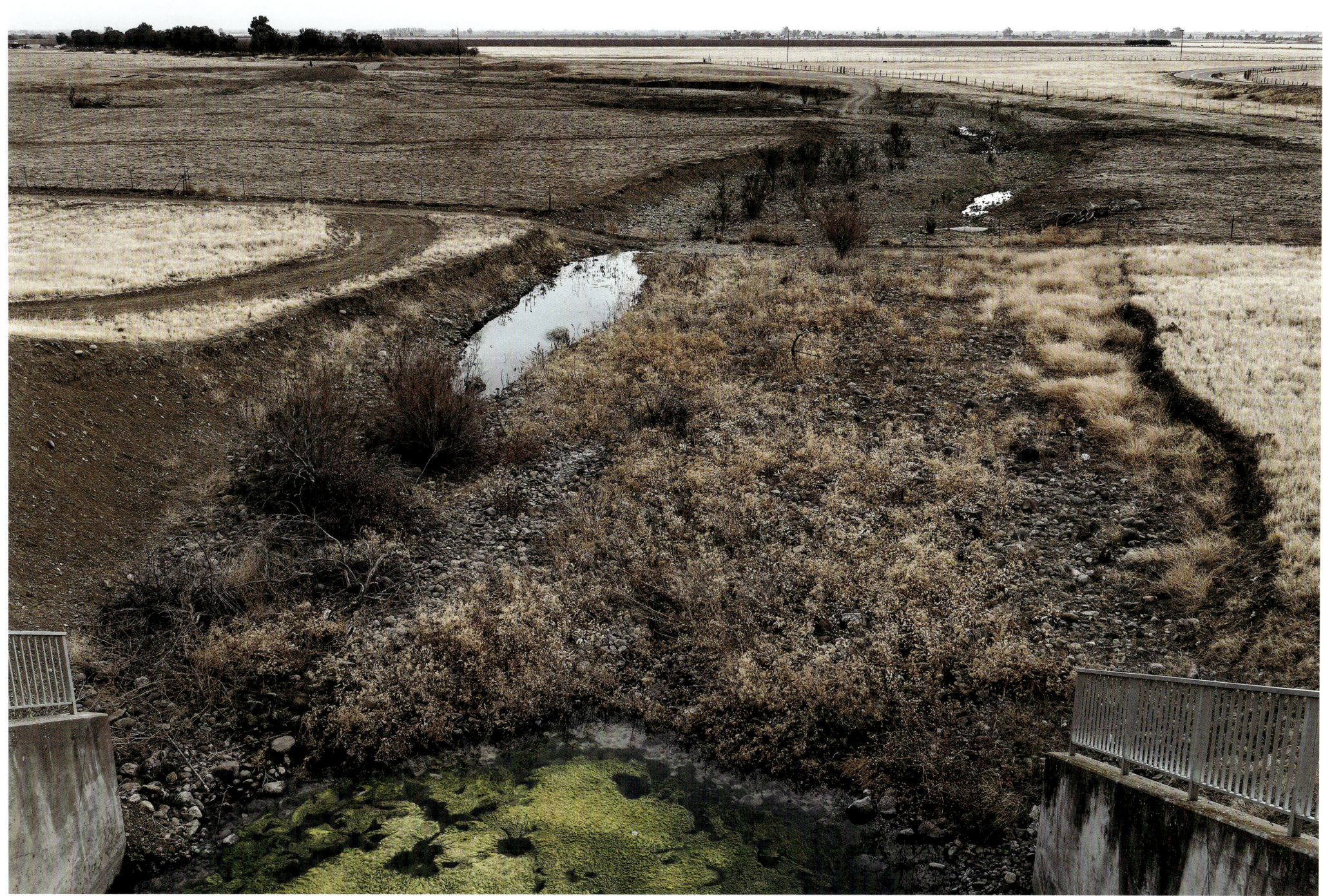

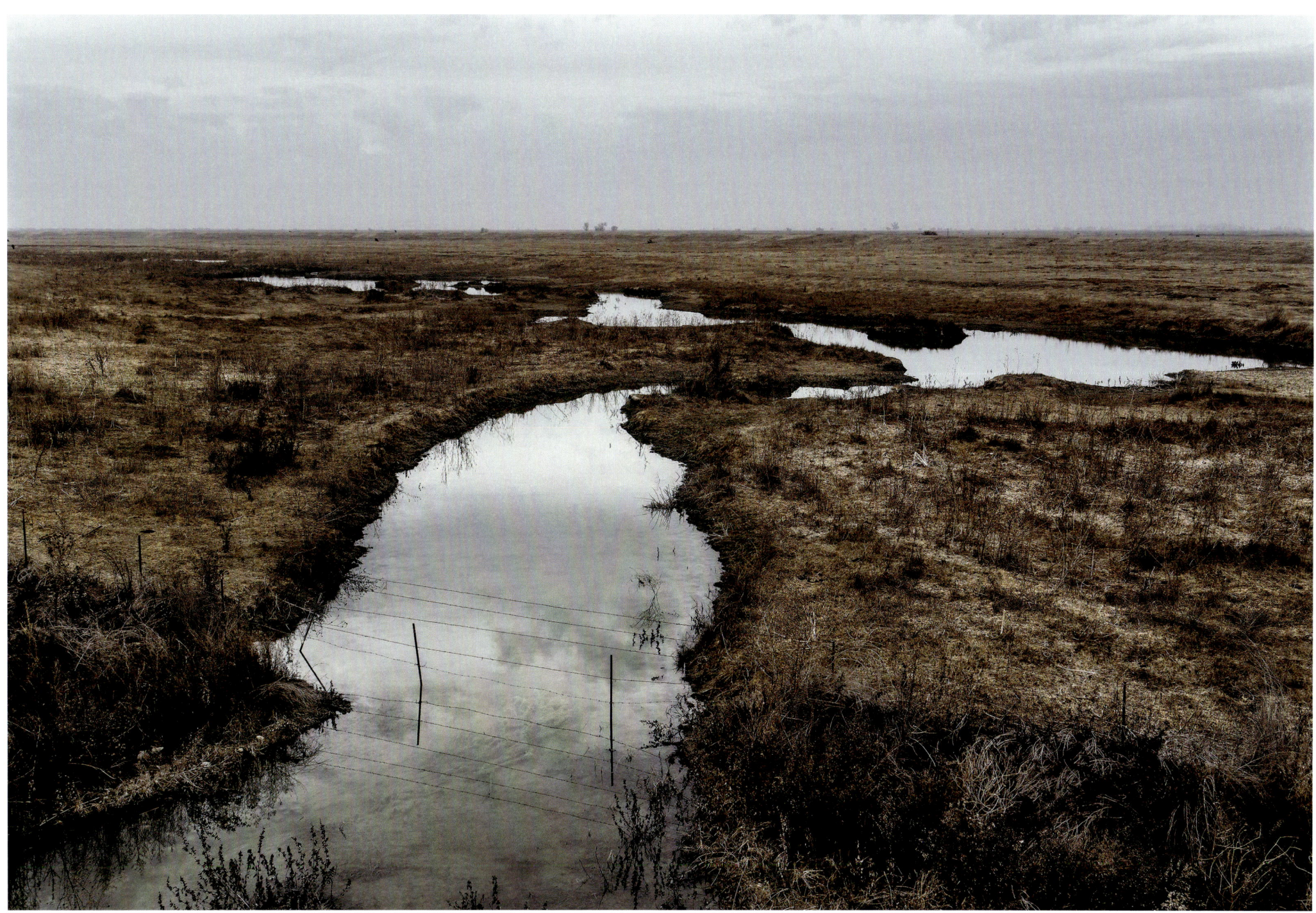

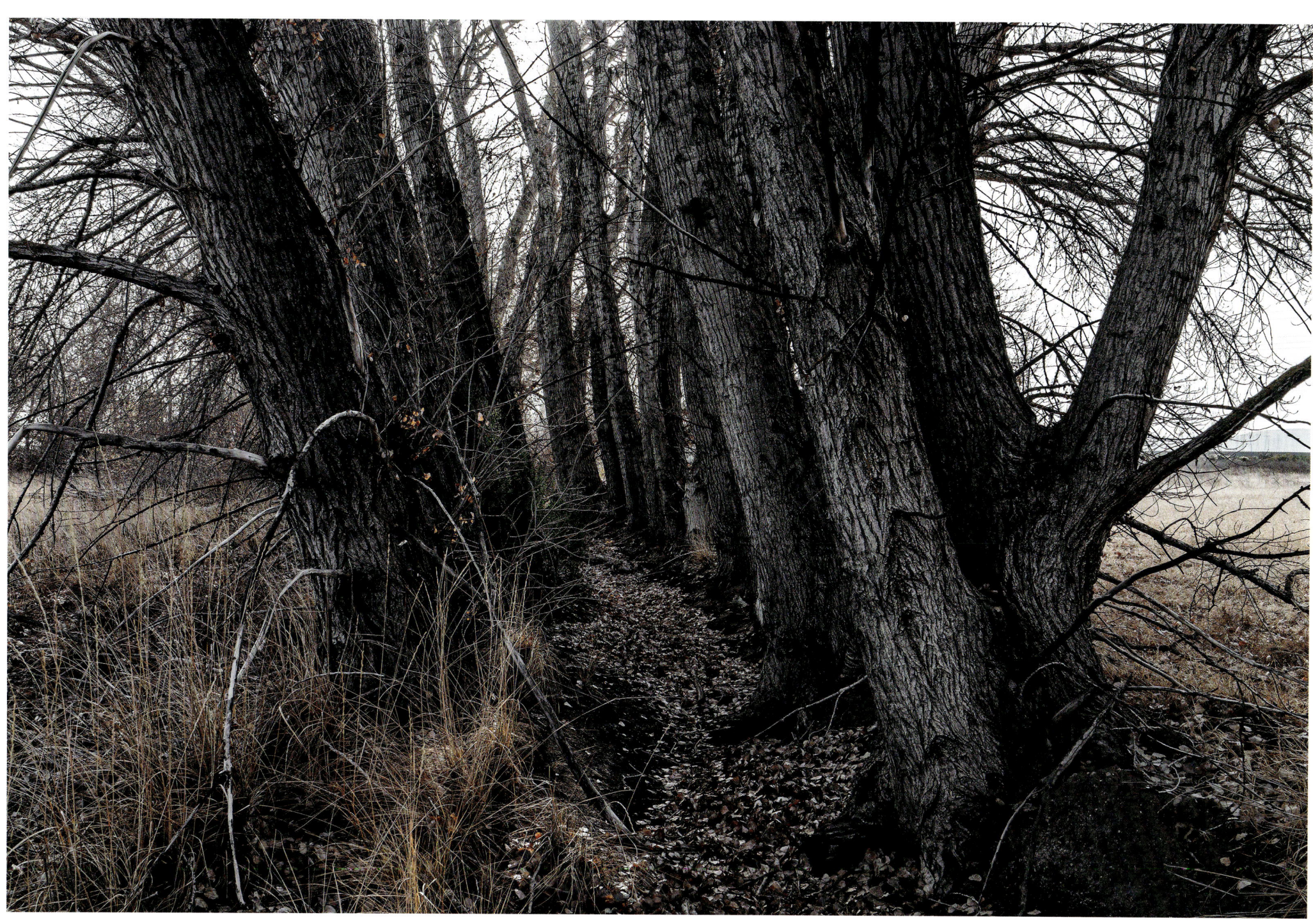

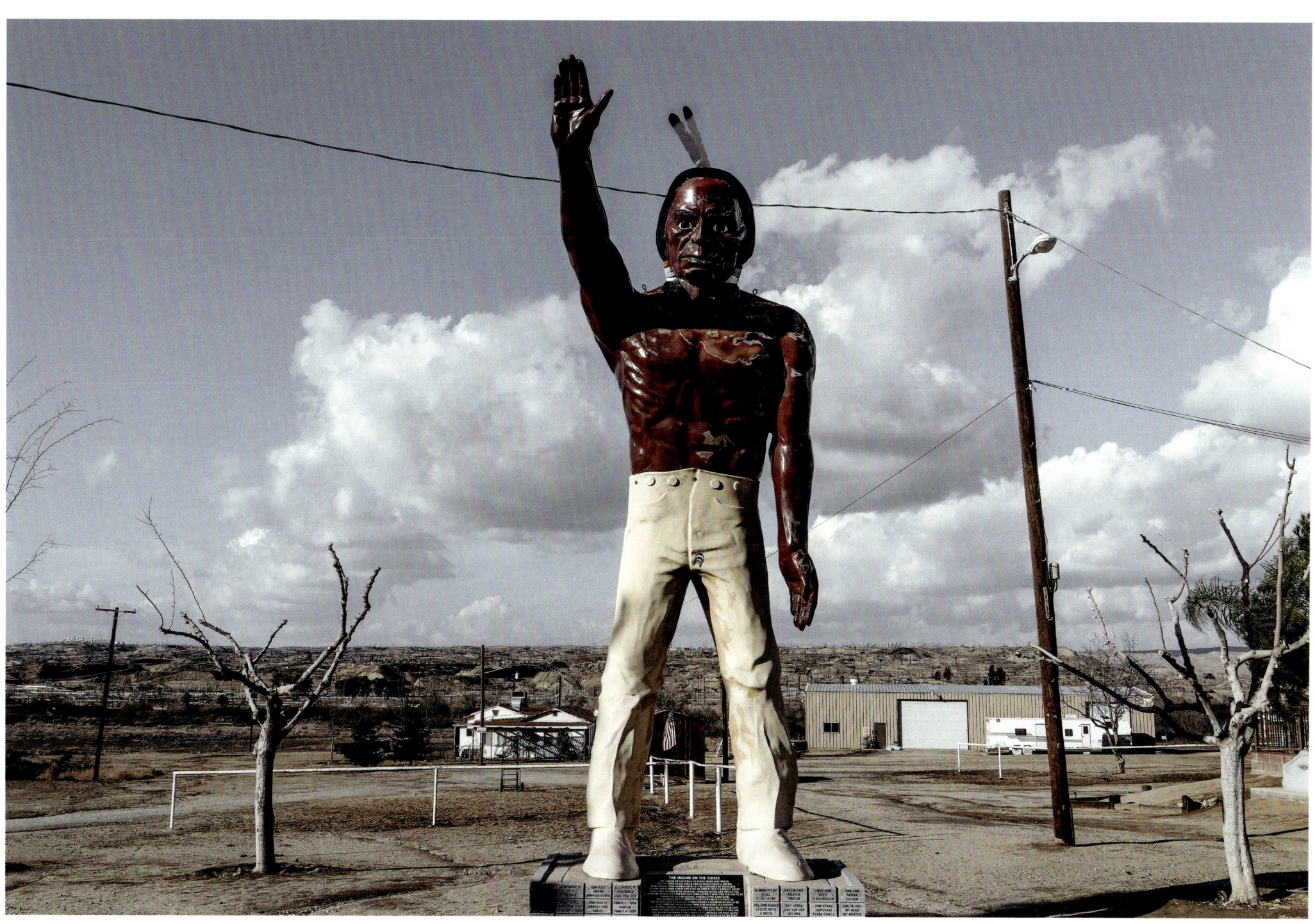

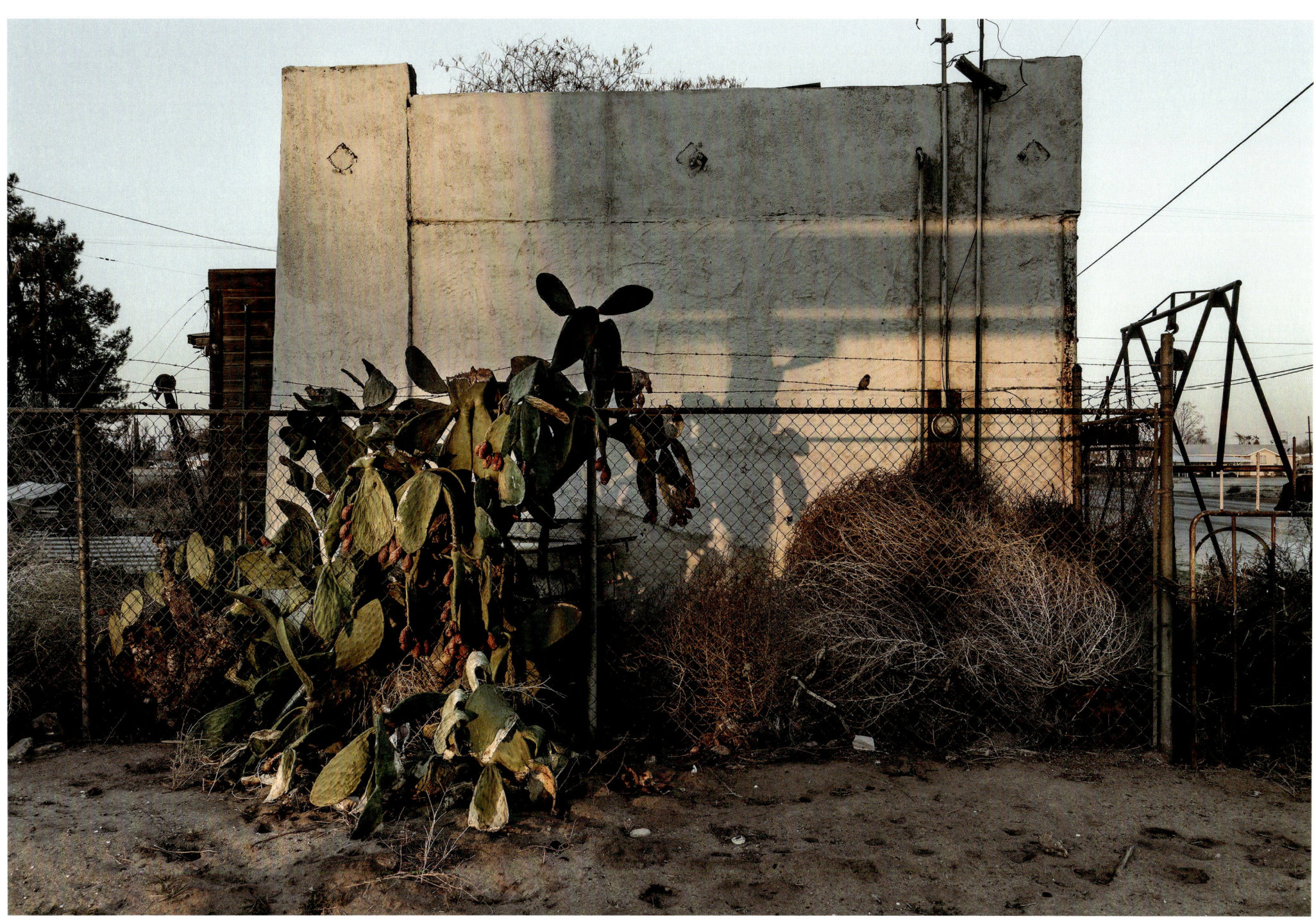

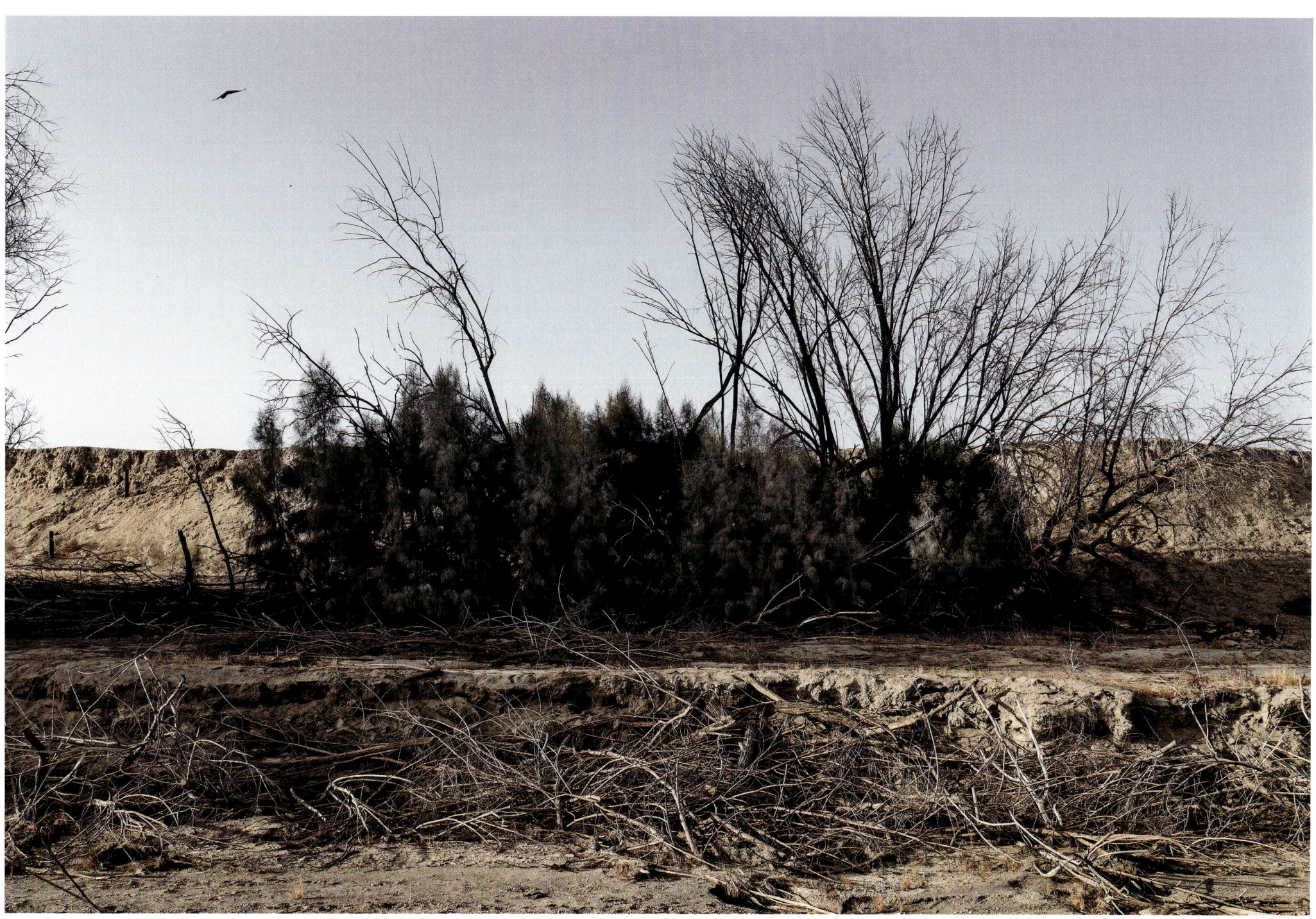

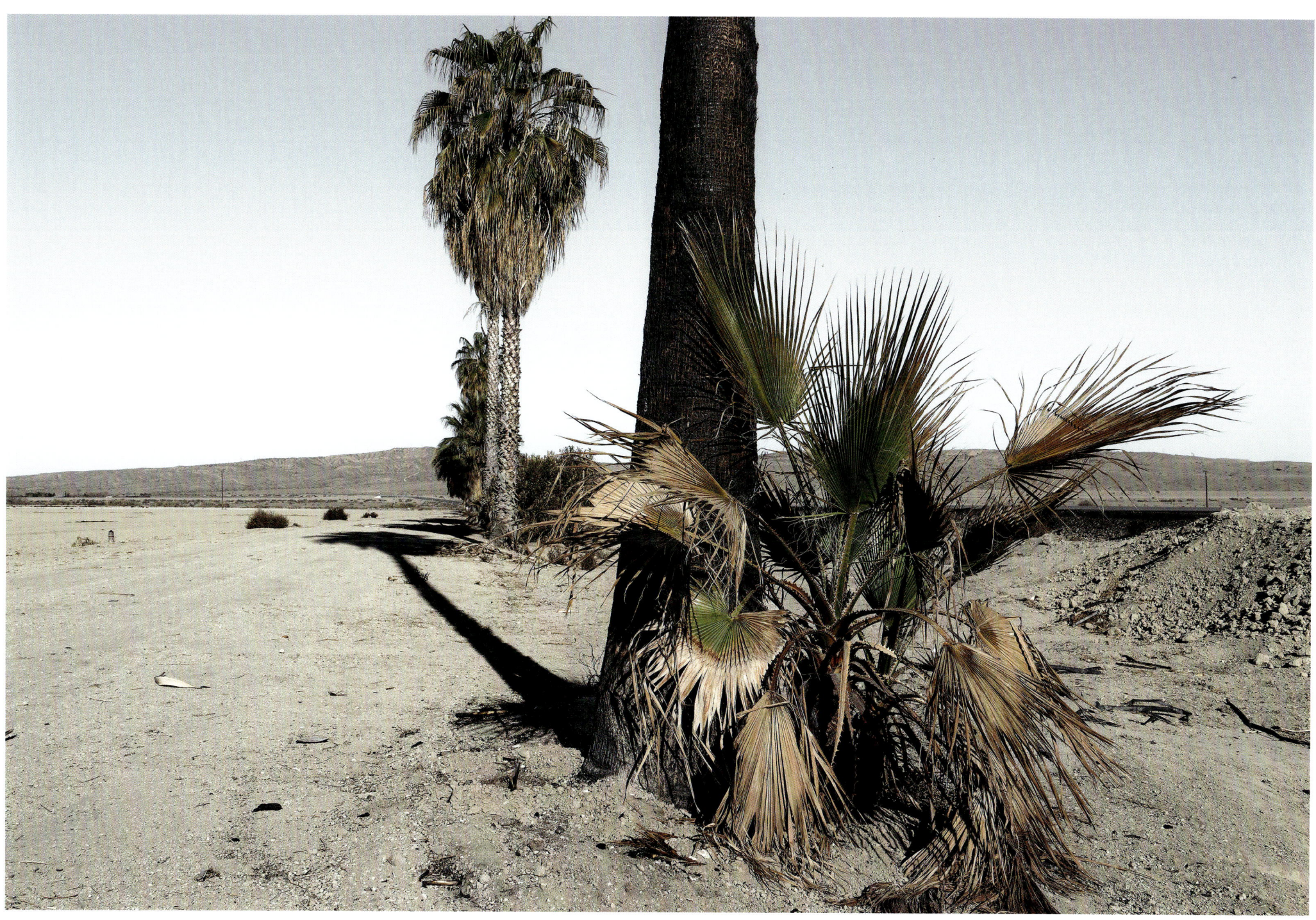

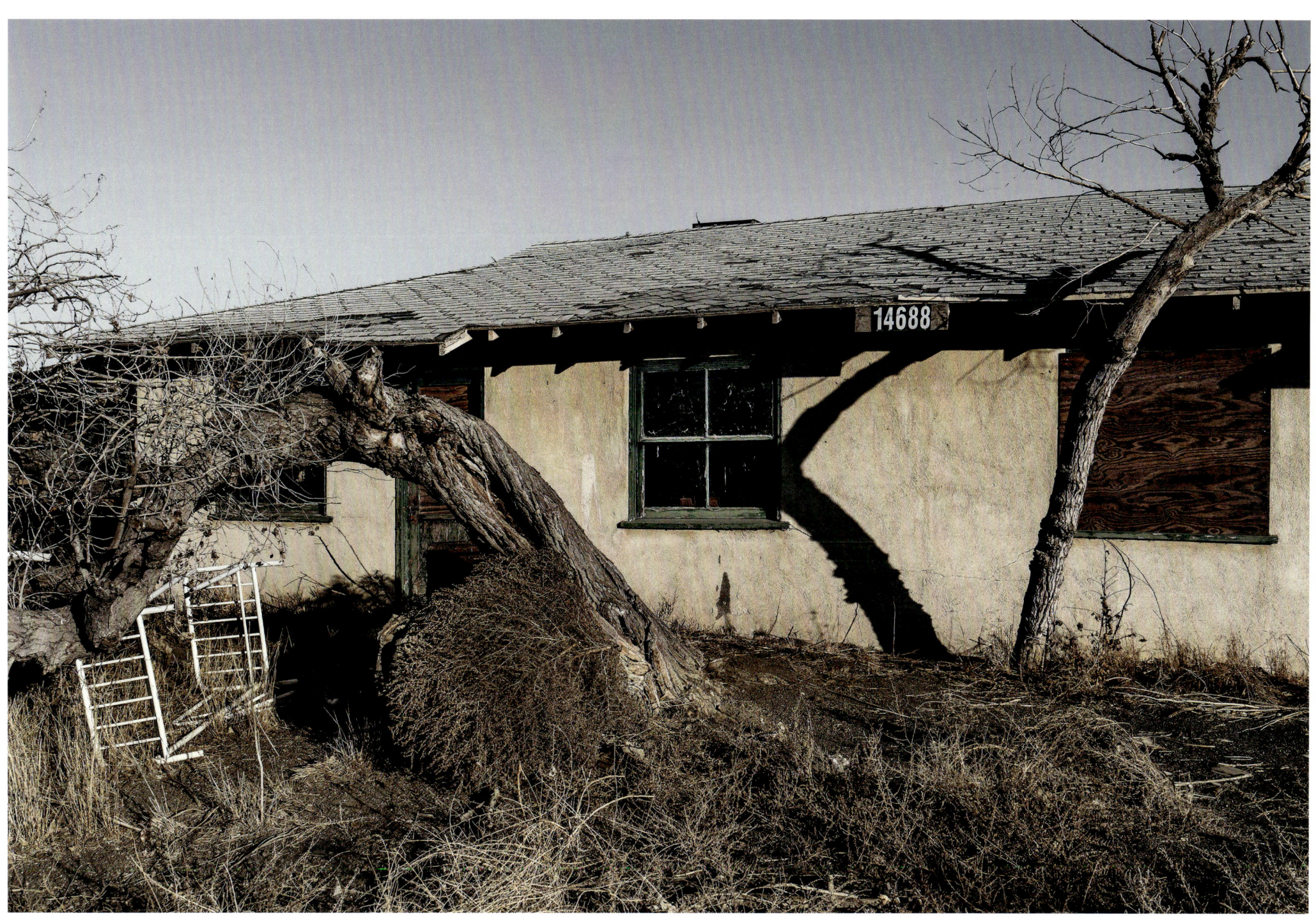

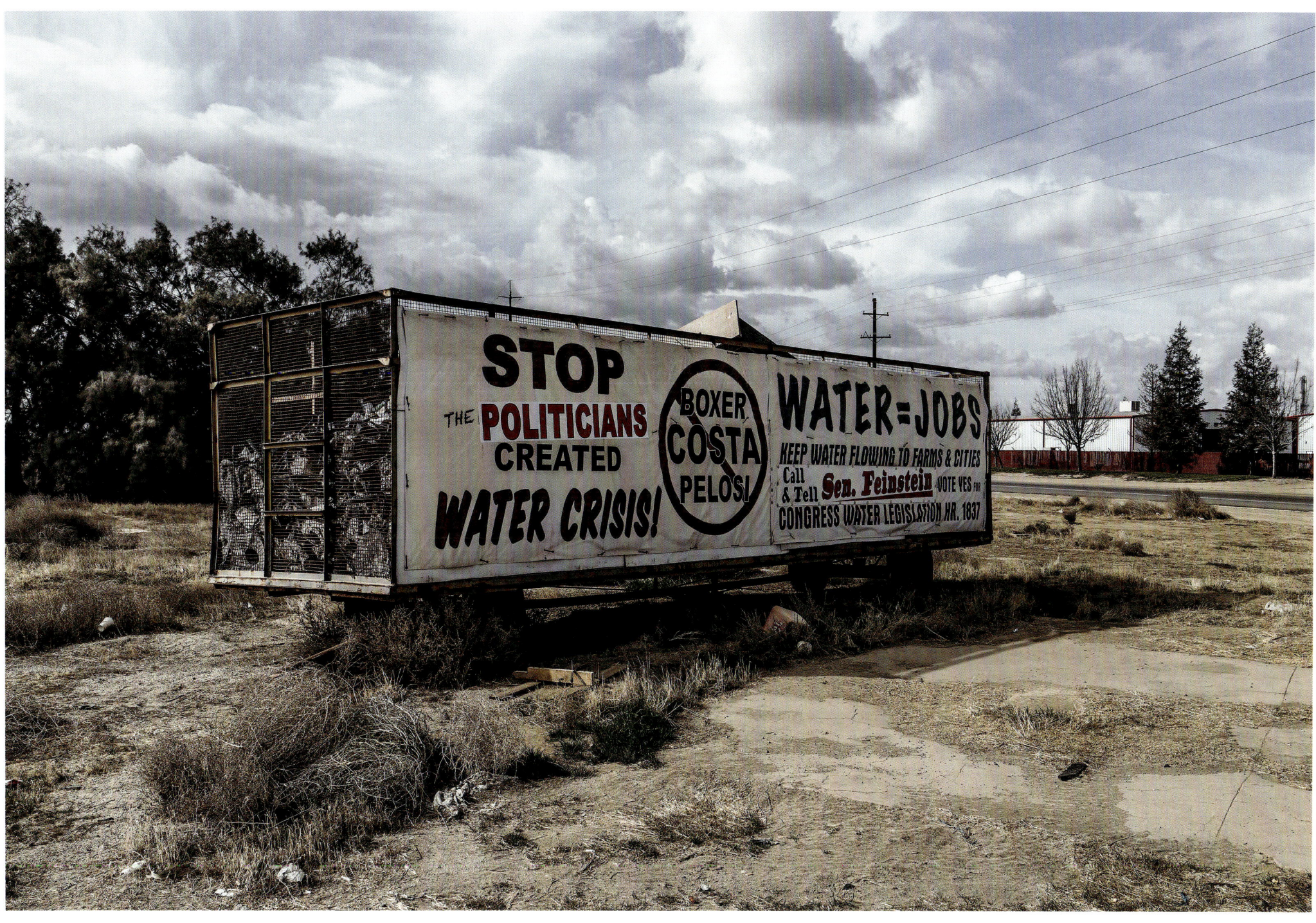

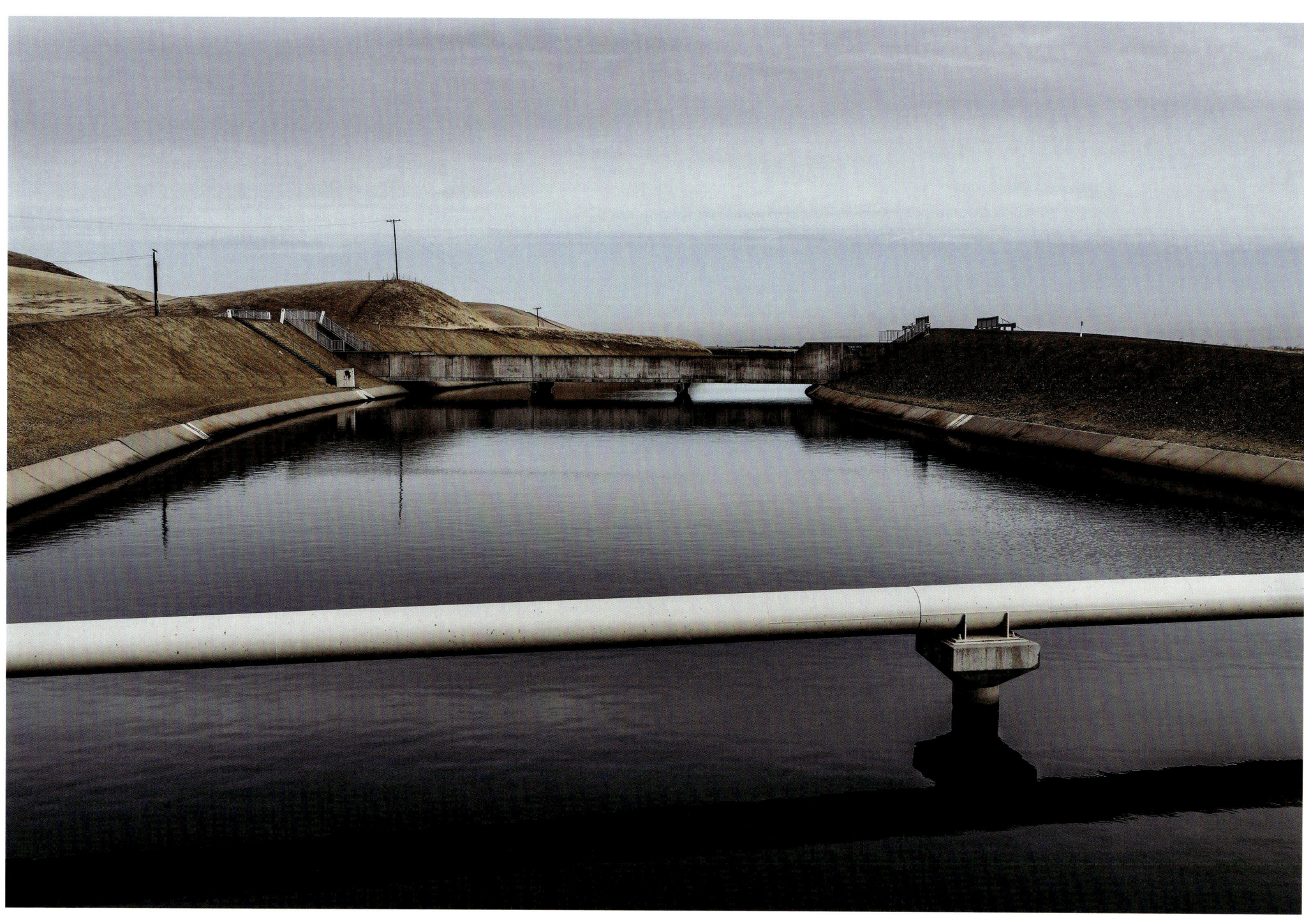

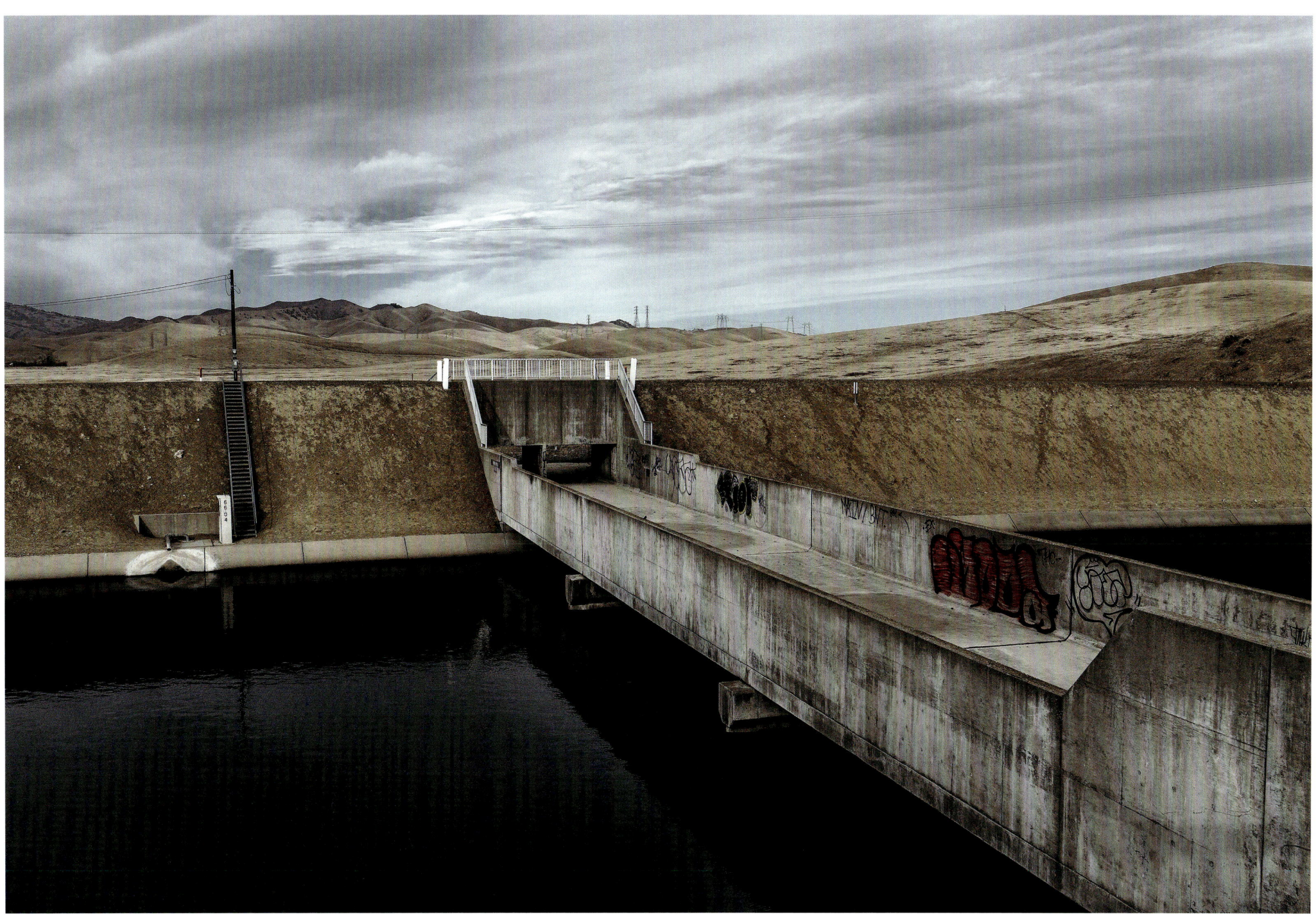

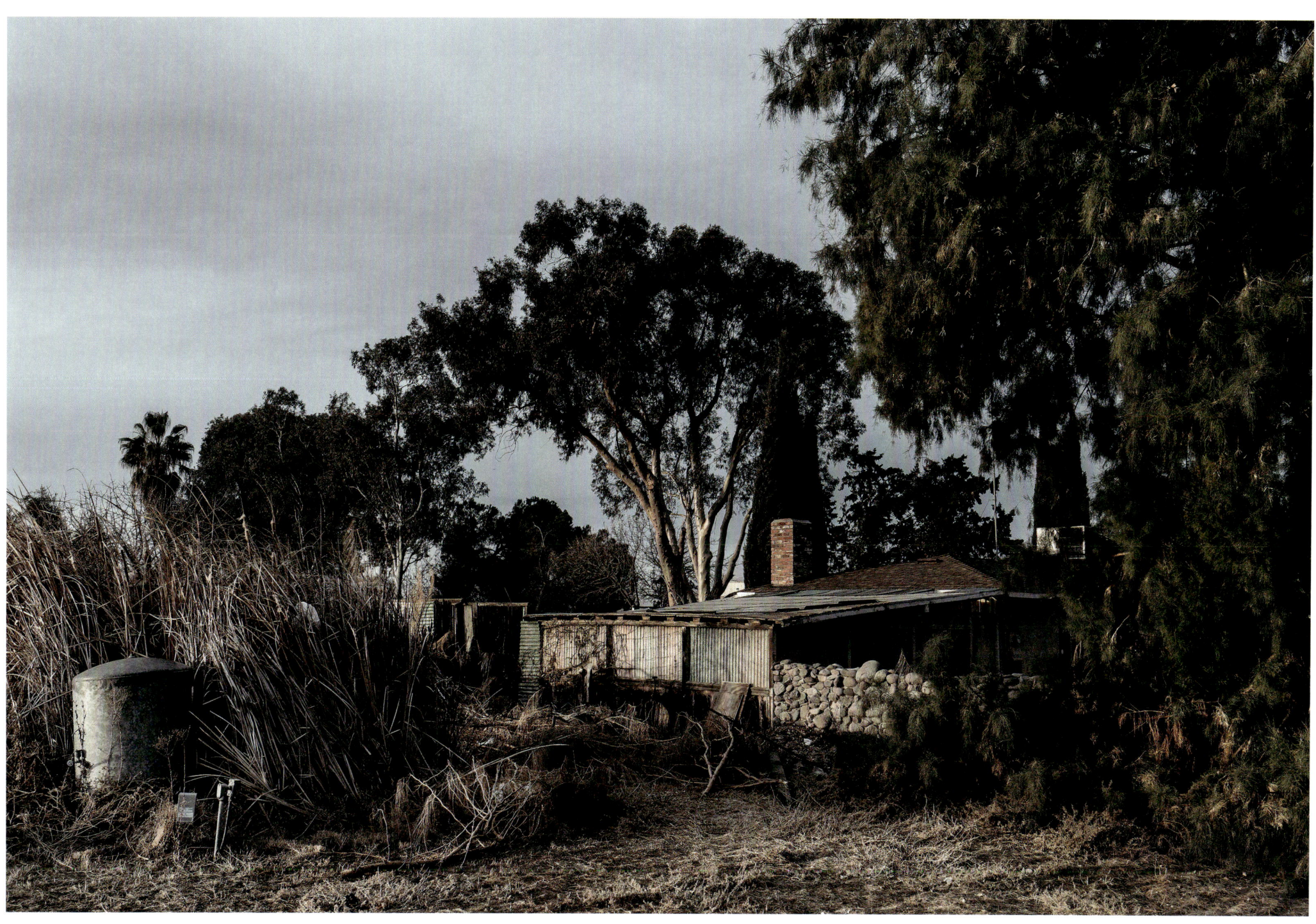

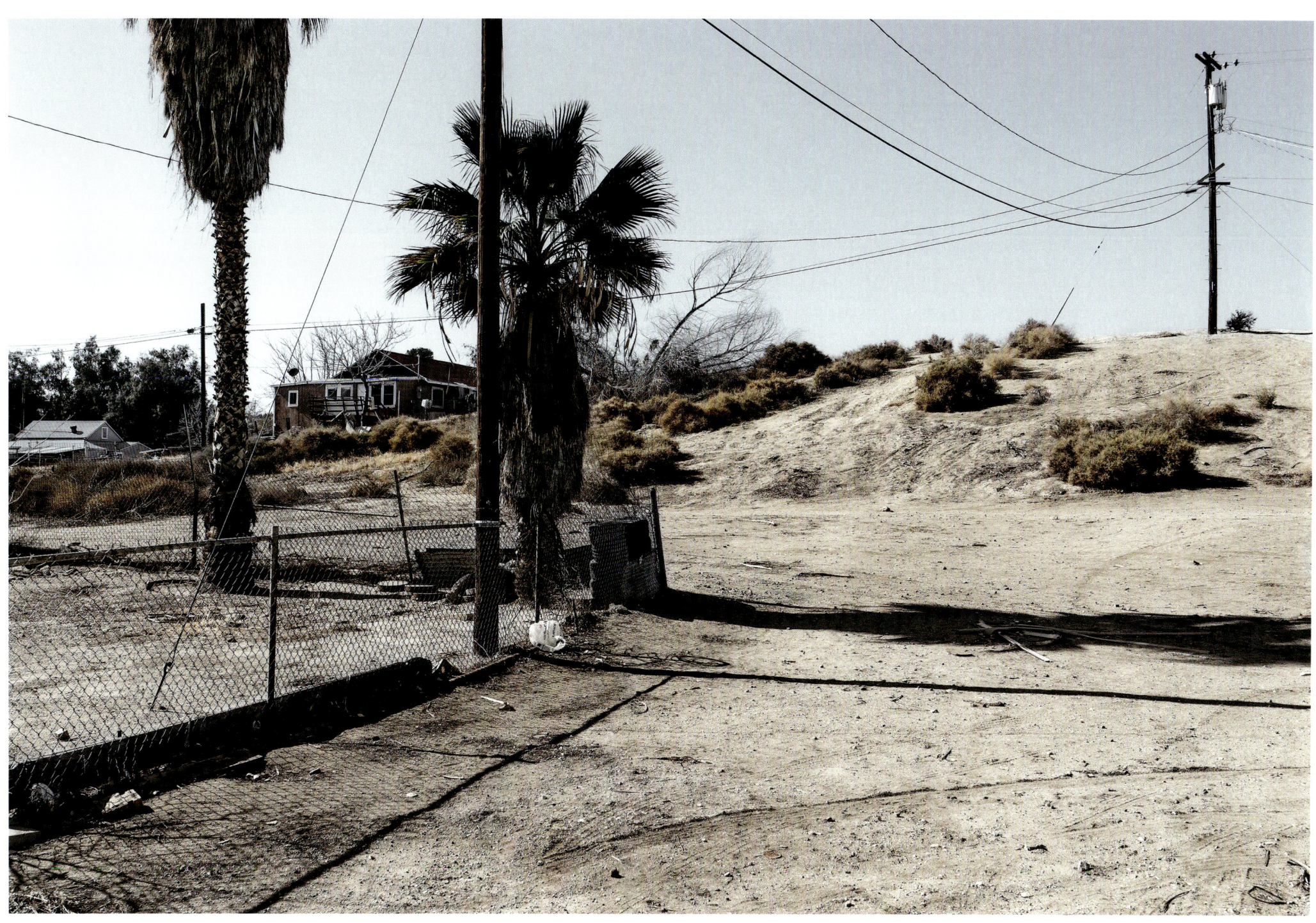

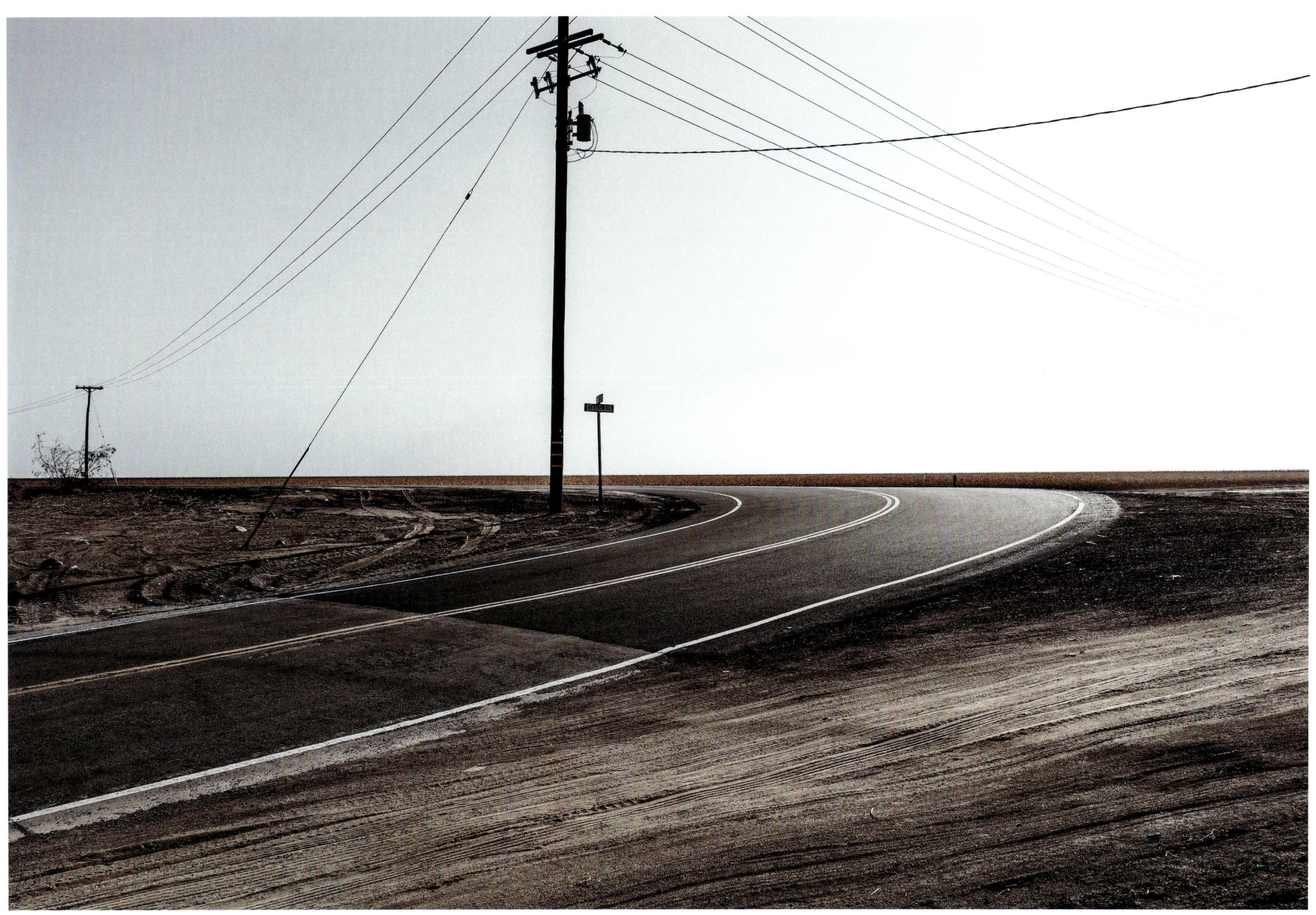

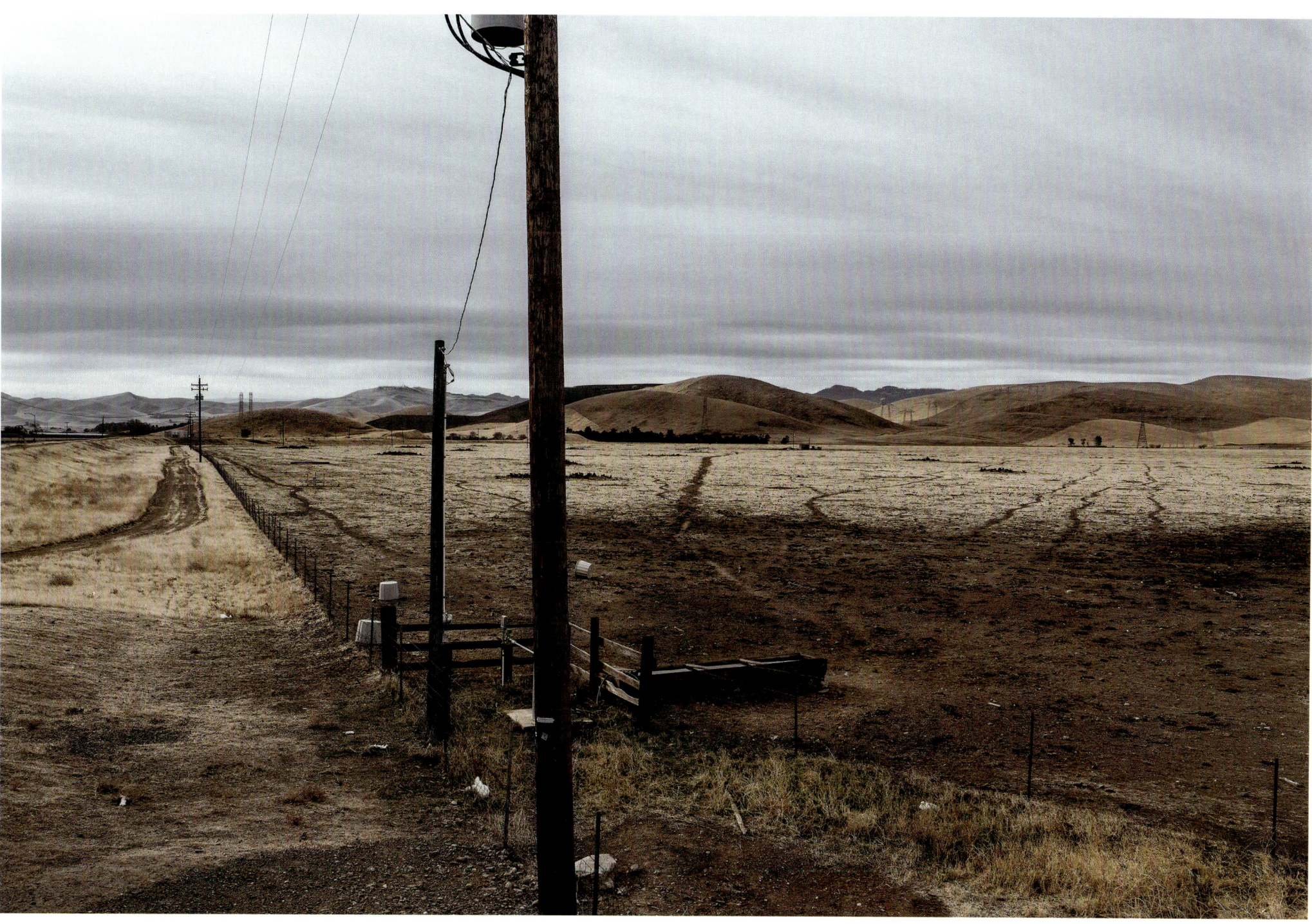

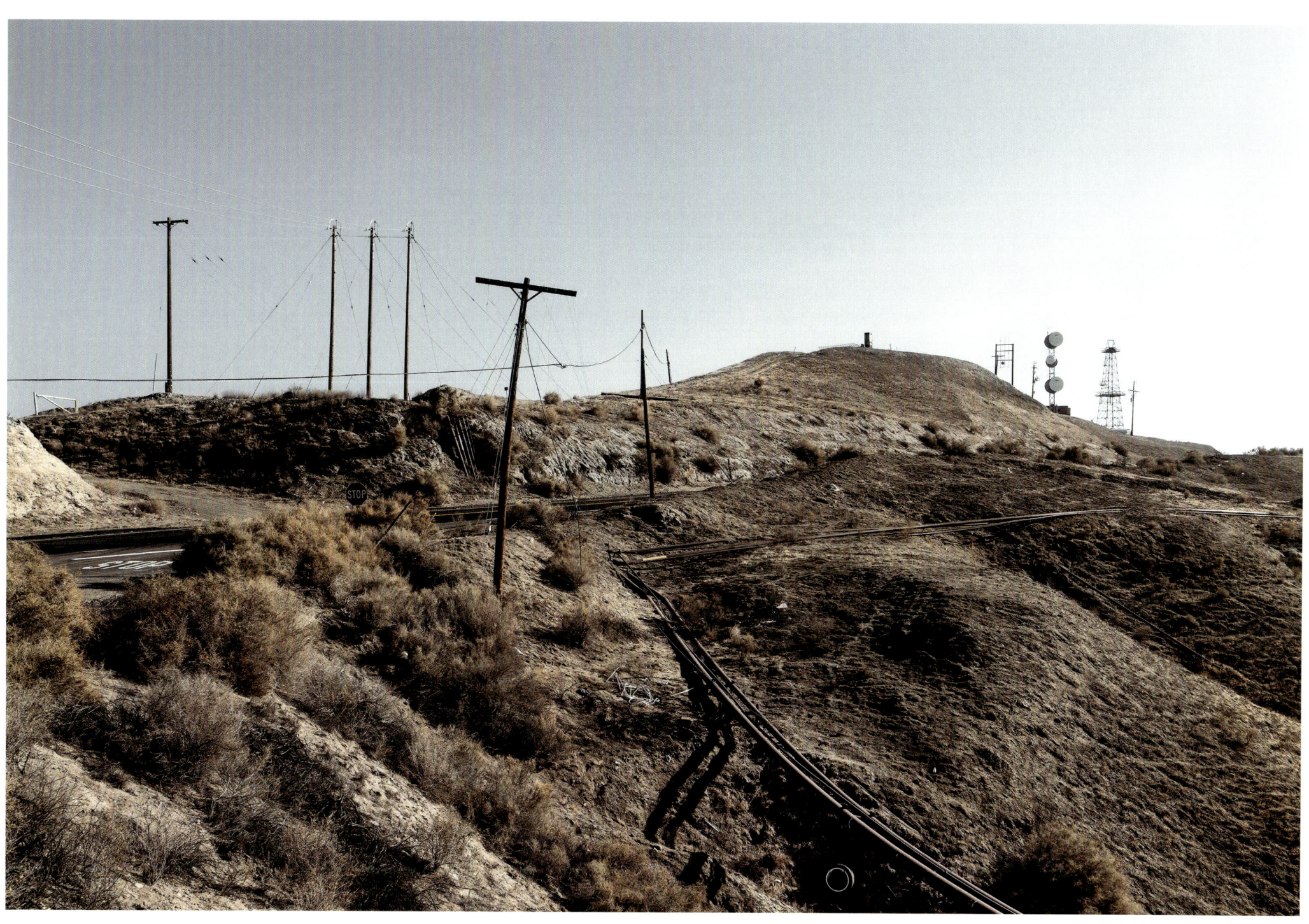

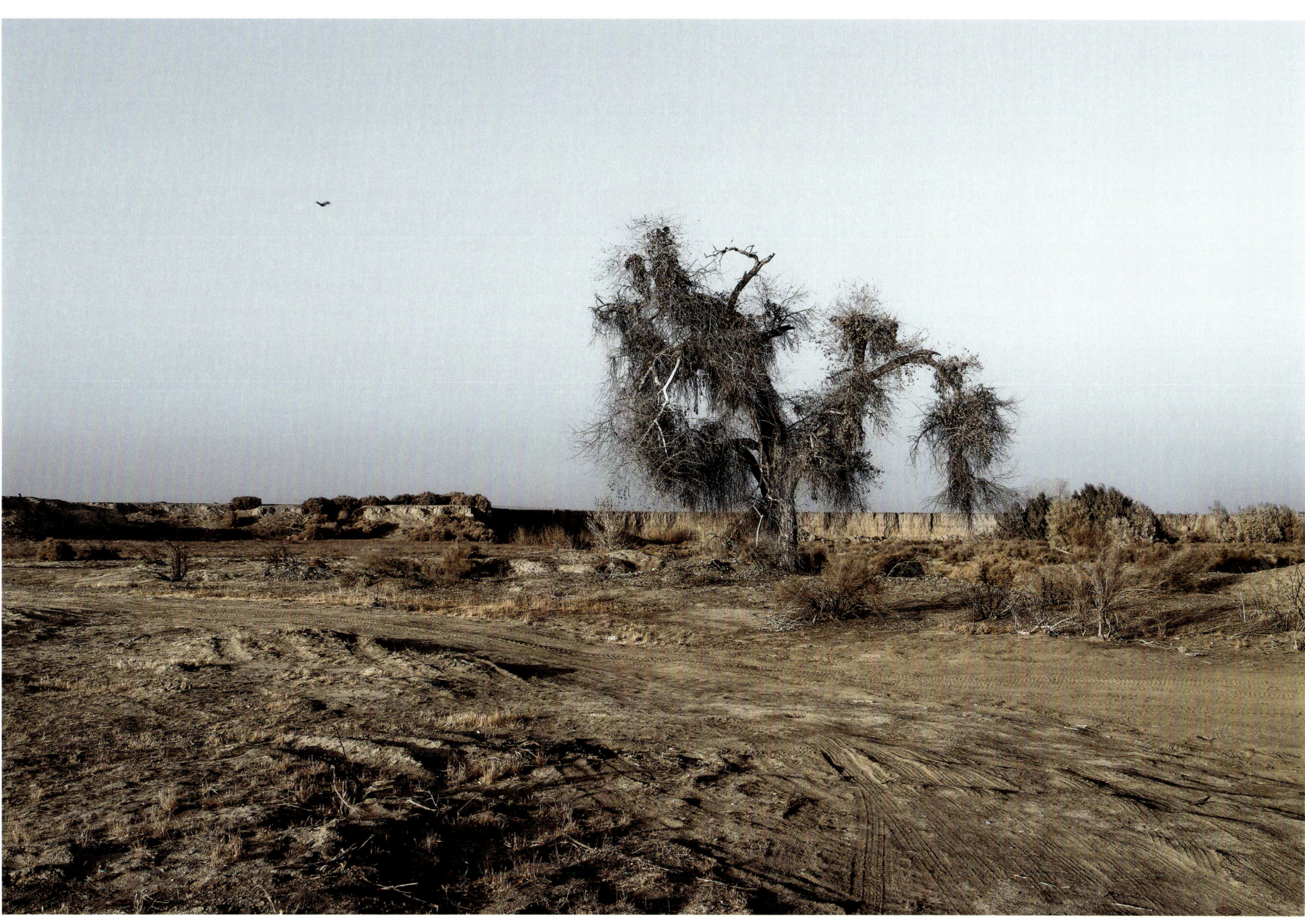

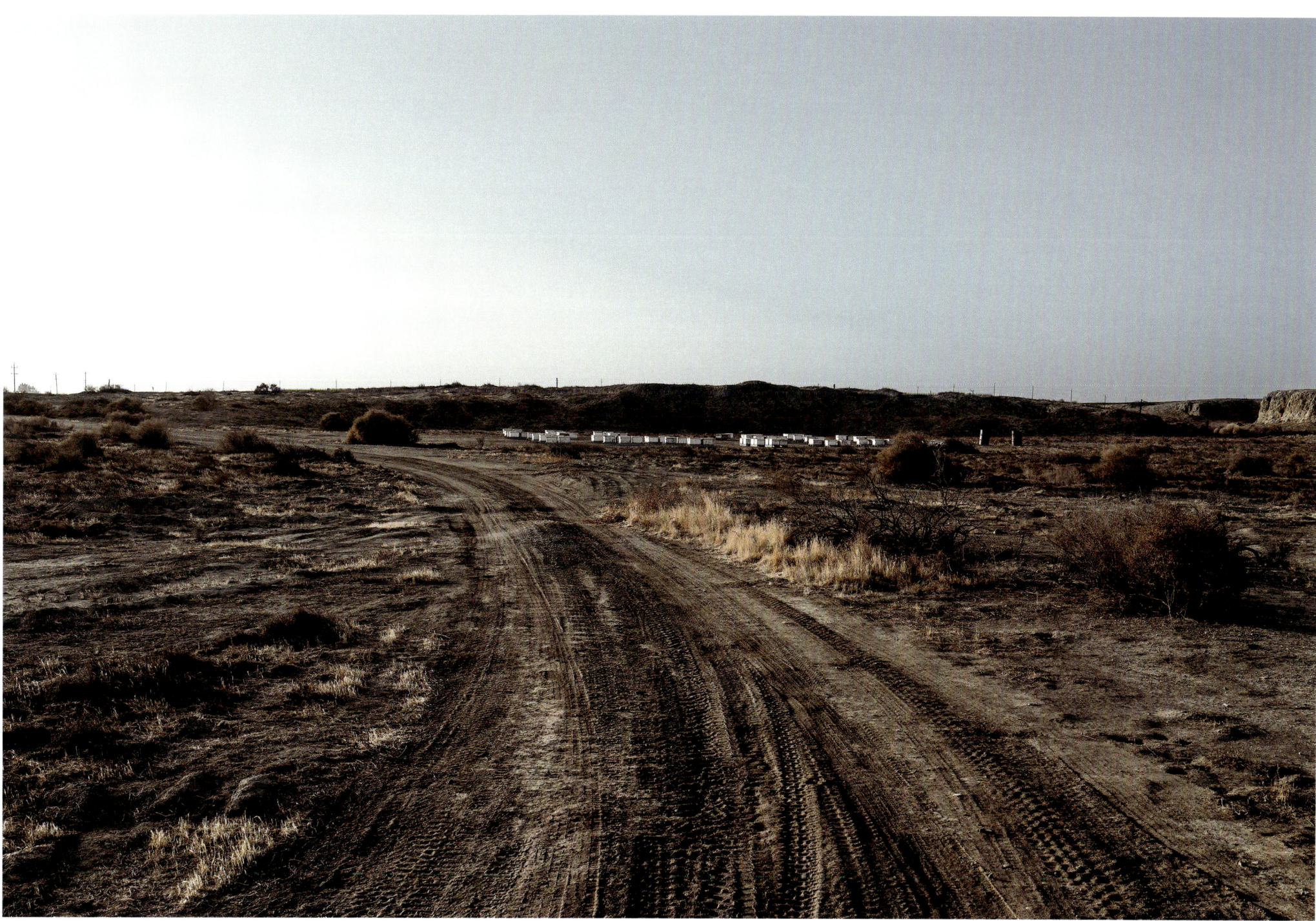

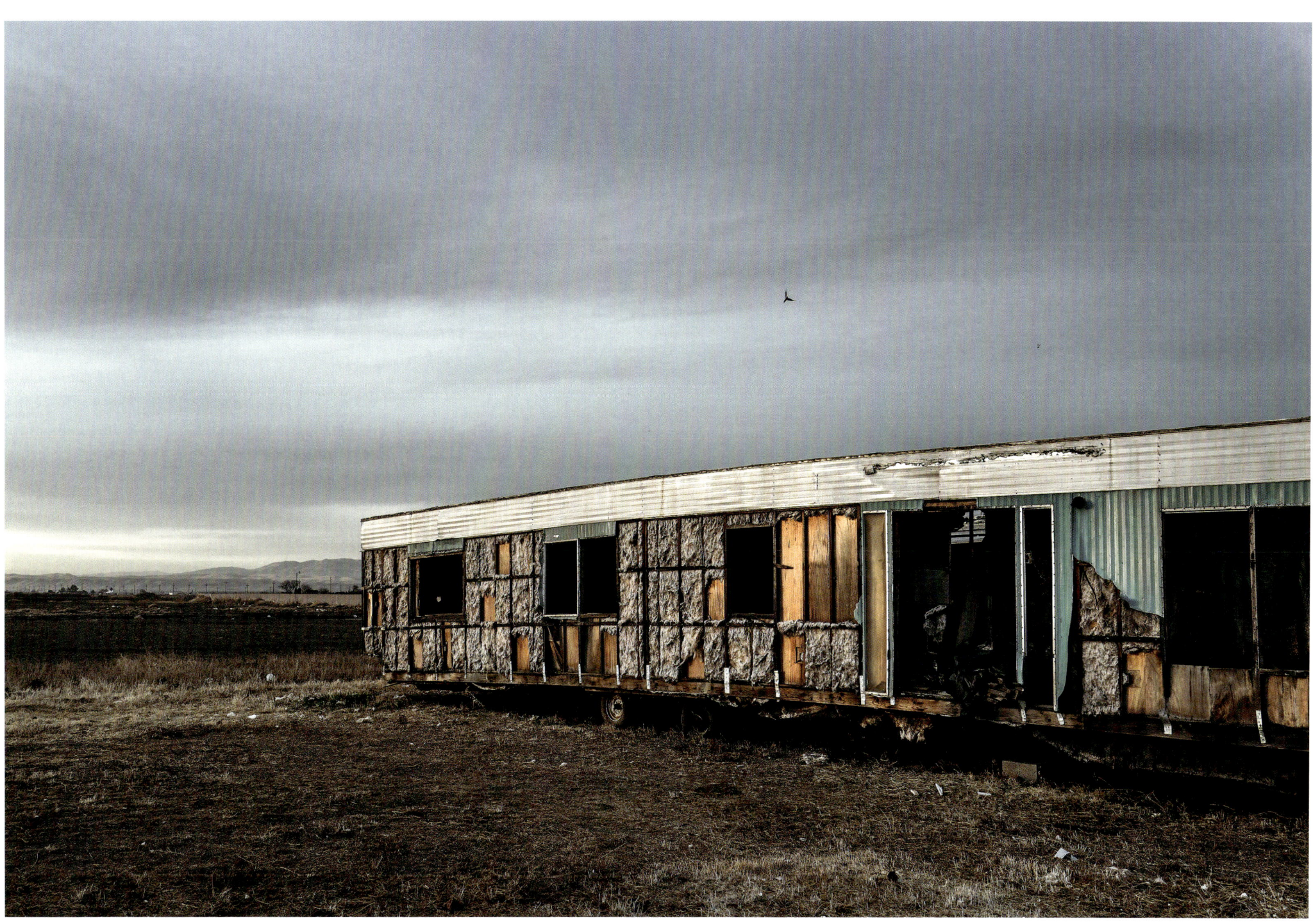

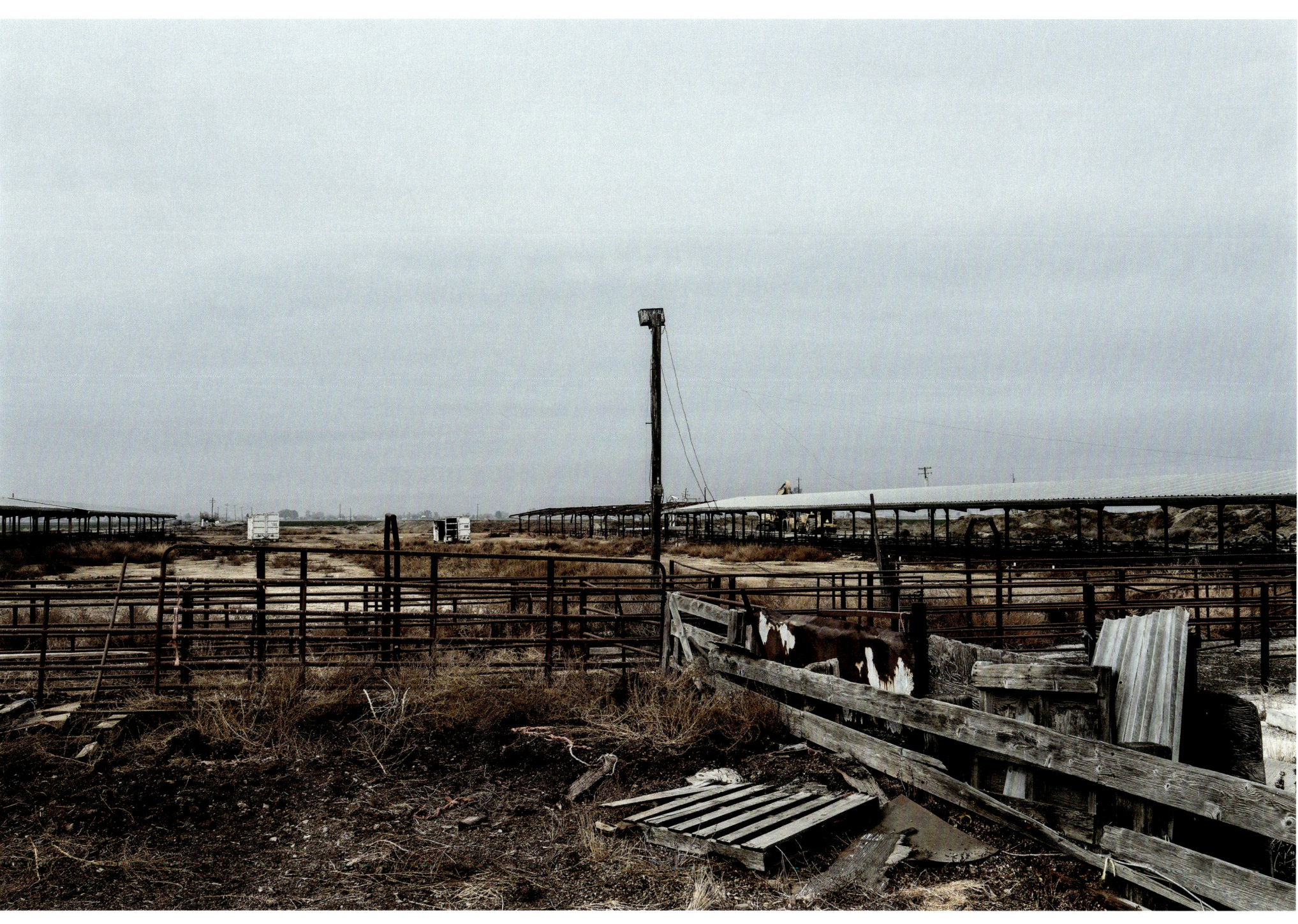

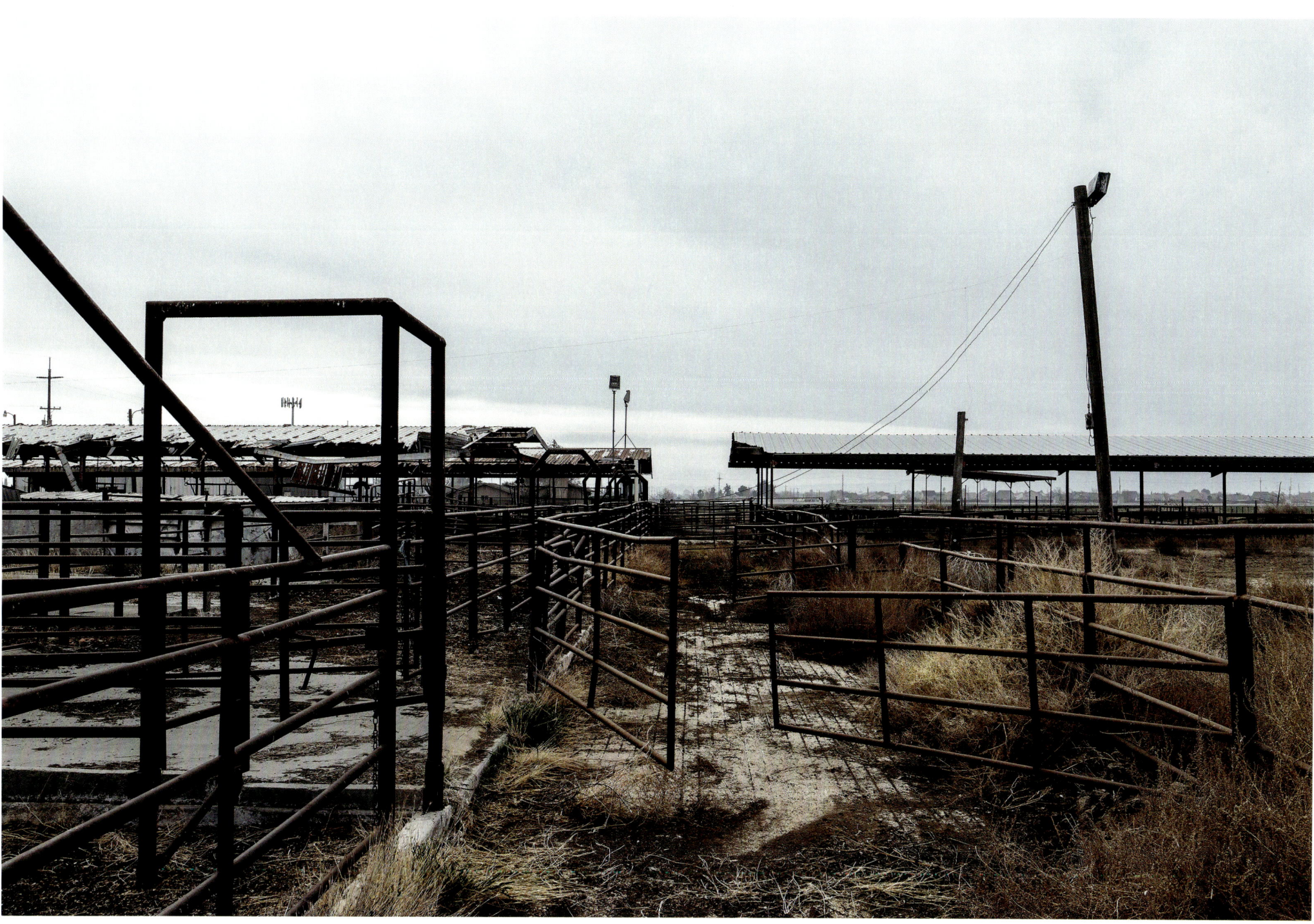

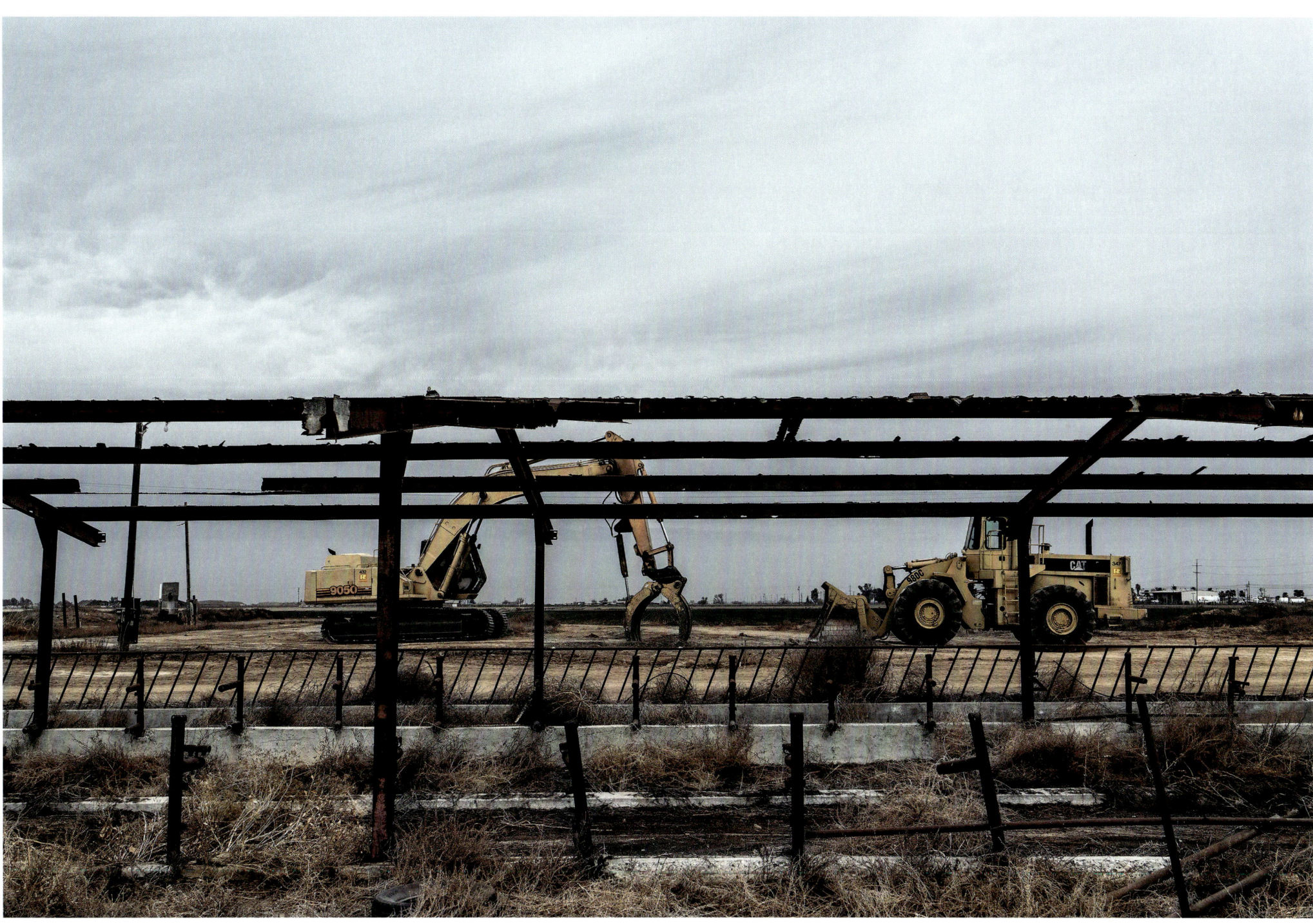

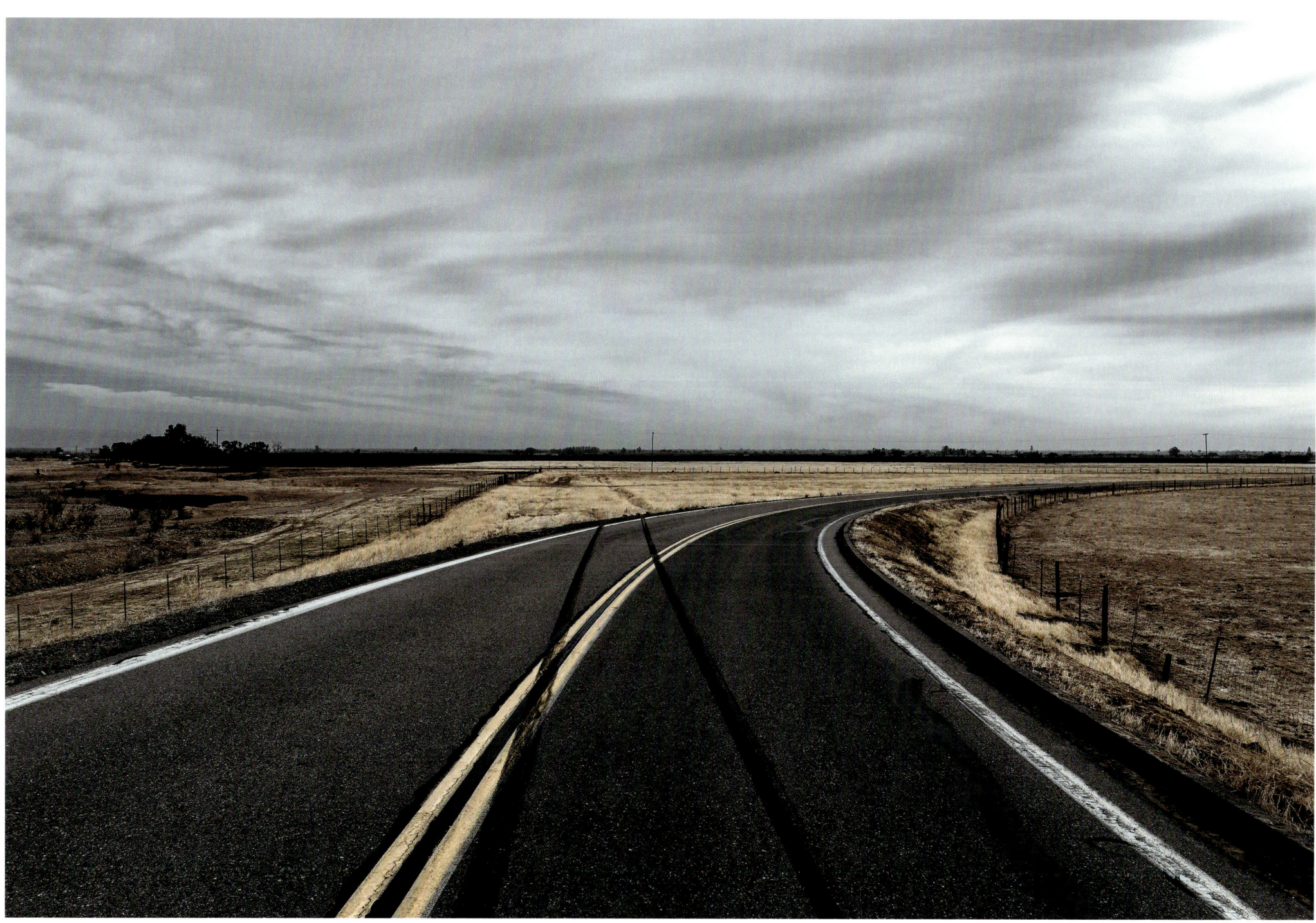

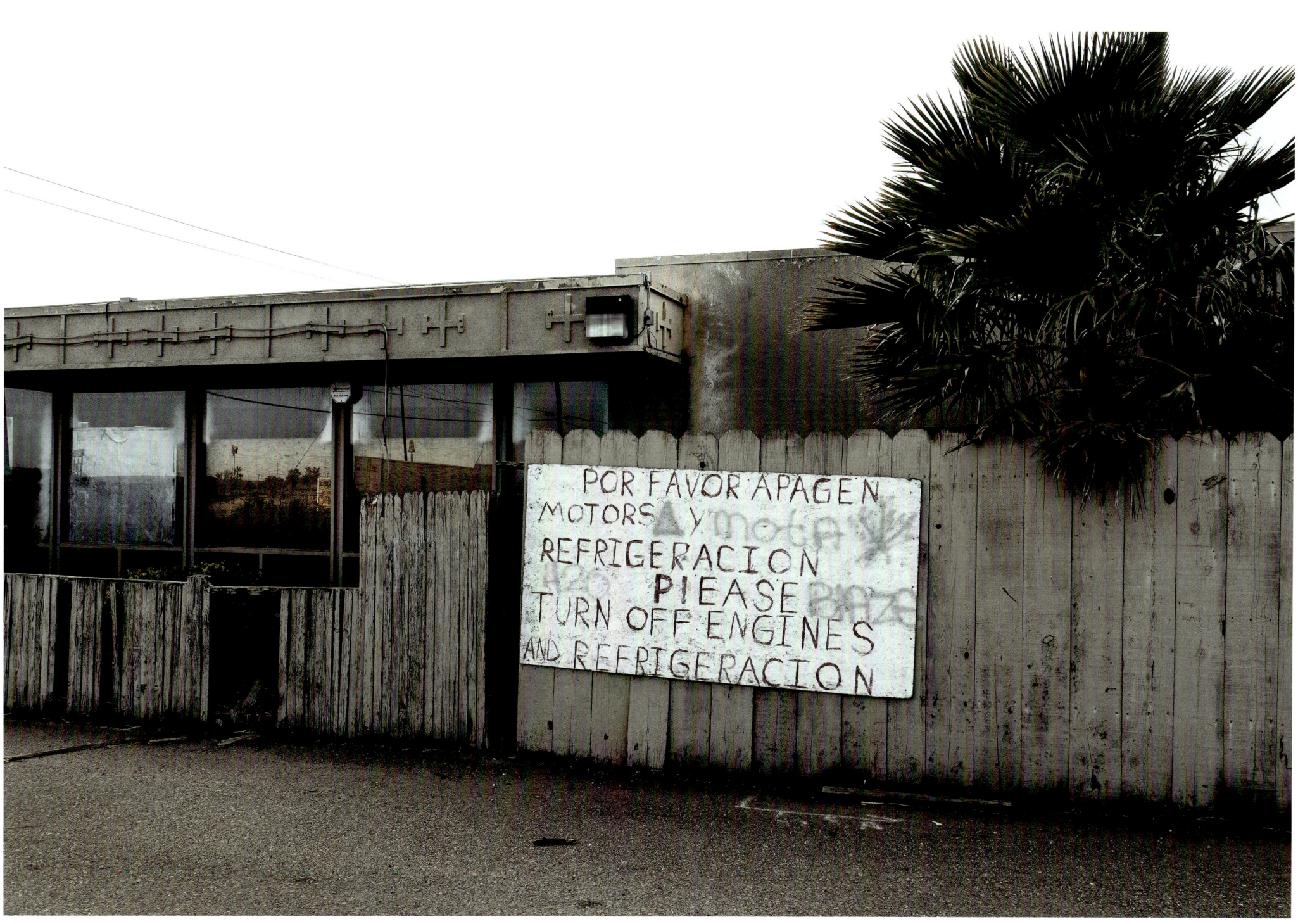

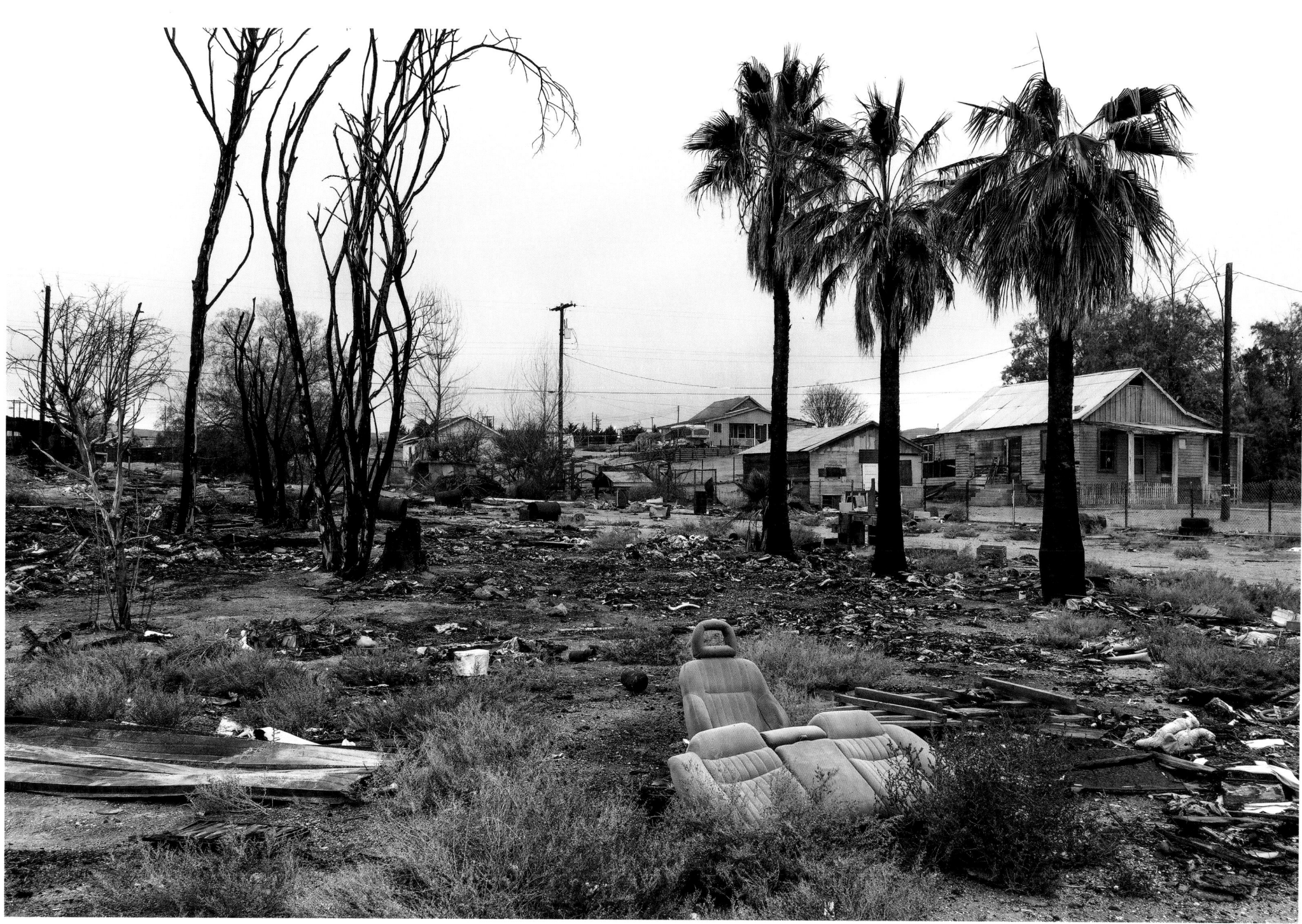

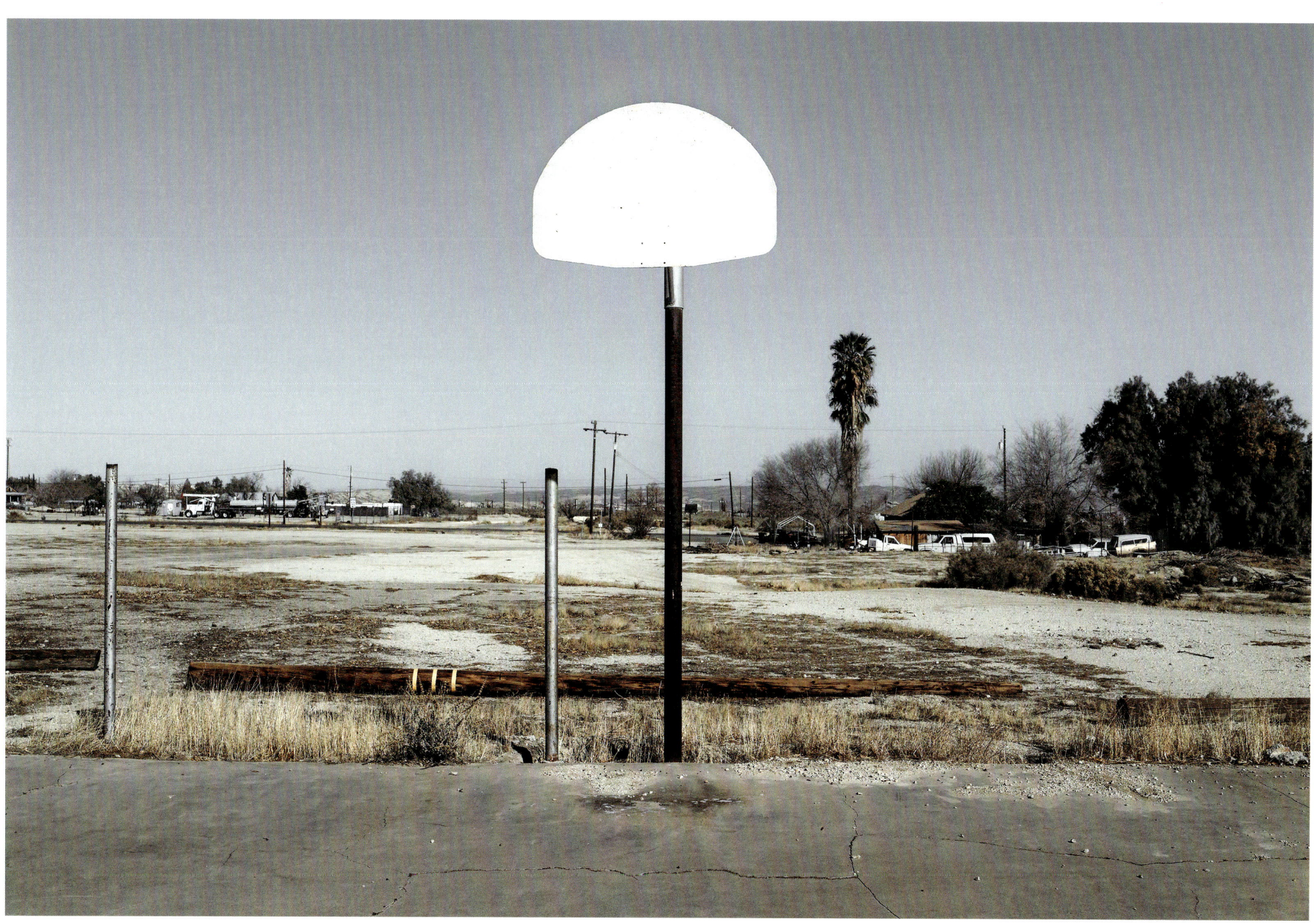

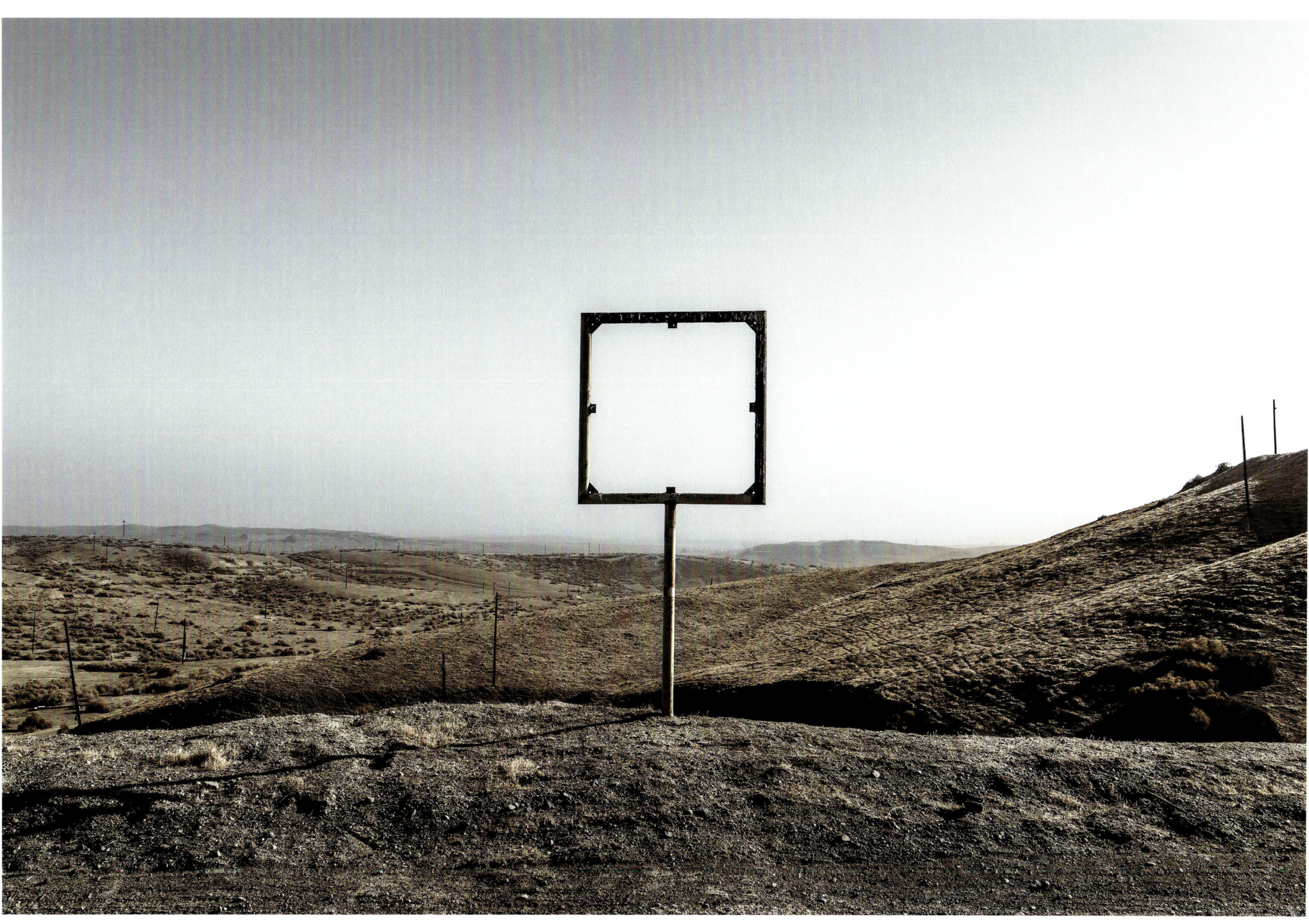

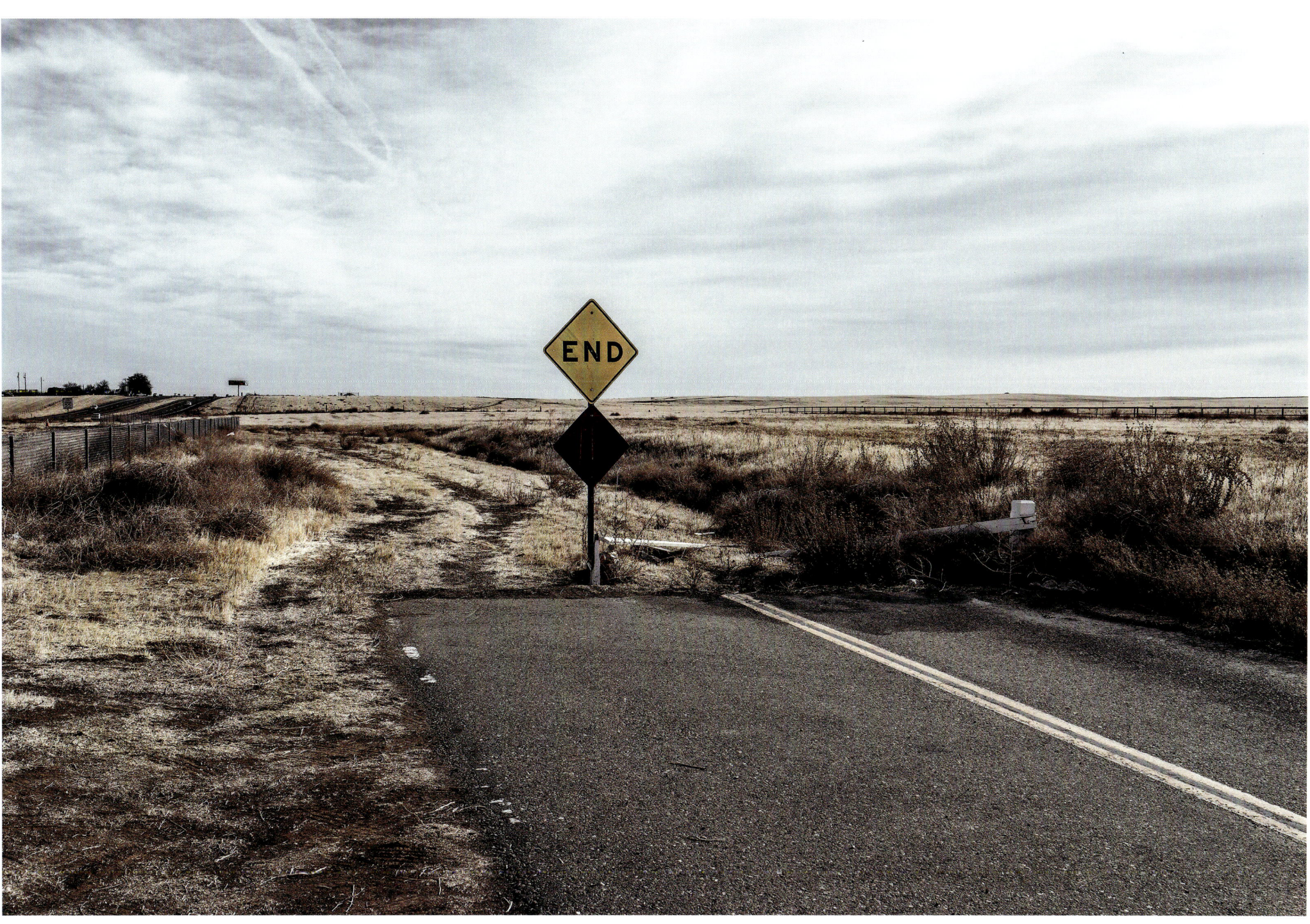

GENETICS OF PLACE

by Kirsten Rian

Sixty-five million years ago, where the San Joaquin Valley now sits, granite slammed into granite, shifted and pushed its way up through the earth's surface, forming mountains and creasing the land at the base of those towering peaks, creating a place for rivers to flow with runoff and sediment. Within that basin, one of the most fertile valleys on the planet was formed.

A series of tectonic processes molded and remolded the underlying structure of the plates that held the soil in its palm. A repository of rocks filled the inland sea, still nutrient-rich with marine and Paleozoic sediments. That from before imprints on that which is to come, even in geology.

Bruce Haley spent his formative years on a small ranch in the southwestern portion of the San Joaquin Valley, in an area between Lemoore and Riverdale known as the Island District. Not the sort of young man who was easily contained indoors (setting a pattern that would last a lifetime), he ran the land, rode horses and dirt bikes across the fields, and grew up.

The land holds memories and footsteps that, while washed away or covered up with new growth, or pavement, or crops, are still there underneath it all. Somewhere.

Haley has walked a lot of earth, and won awards for the way his camera accompanied him along the way, from Burma to Romania to Nevada, where it's possible to wander and never be found. He has anchored his life in the land, now under vast and unpredictable sky in another valley, this time in the far northeastern corner of California.

You reach a certain age and the inventory of experience—of people who have passed through, some staying, some not—and of plans made and lost and seen through is a long one. There is an inevitable culling, and looking back and then forward and then back again, reorienting, reorganizing, realigning to correct the dead ends and roadblocks on the map we began drawing of ourselves back in childhood.

It's difficult, perhaps the hardest, fiercest choice of all, to look at the truth. Because truth changes, sometimes daily, and it's exhausting to keep up with the contextual shifts and altered meanings when we see more of what surrounded us, from parents who we hope tried their best, to the reconciling of our own mistakes and misjudgments, all of which stack and accumulate to land us exactly right where we are. It could be worse, it could be better. And that's the truth.

The truth of the San Joaquin Valley is crowded cities, strip malls, abandoned buildings, farm debt, and dust. It's also still fertile with Class 1 soil, and the major roadways buzz with truck traffic carrying massive amounts of agricultural products that feed the rest of America. It's corporate farms and big money, it's small farms and dairies struggling to survive, it's poverty. It's generations of home and family, it's migration out and away, and immigration law ensnarement. And that's the truth.

We humans and our history are riddled with dichotomies; we spend the years of our lives reconciling while navigating that space between the good and the bad, the sad and the happy, the dreams and realities.

****

The rivers and tributaries lace and interlace, knot up, dry out, flood, and leave their mark. In good years—in good decades—the crops are green and lush and abundant. Irrigation snakes its way as man-made streams mirroring the earth's, flowing, abundant, life-giving. In hard years, dust particles veil the valley and blur the view out across the horizon—out across what one thinks they see, have always seen or known.

Every day begins with a line. Sometimes, through the smog, or early dawn haze, it's a blur; other times sharp like a pen line drawn straight across paper. Tire tracks wind and we work to understand the boundaries of home. Across the American West, numberless dreams of the nineteenth century resolved themselves in the San Joaquin Valley. Hammer blow by hammer blow, foot by foot, railroad ties stapled steel to earth. Picks and shovels and sledgehammers rang on metal. This is the thing of myth and legend. Standard-gauge rail line arcs up and over and around, and less than a century later, black lines of asphalt draw themselves up and over and around rows of trees, rows of tilled soil, plow ridge and furrow, crop borders, fence lines, property lines, county lines, bread lines, immigration lines, pipe lines, telephone lines, tree line, skyline, electrical line, assembly line, water line, and always—the only thing that is always—the horizon.

We become invisible.

Then try to make sense of our life by looking at every single thing around us.

Now, this Valley is a place where rain is luck, and politics, fate.

And the truth, like most truths, complicated. Tell it like it is.

Strike-slip motion formed the San Andreas Fault.

Strike the rail tie. Slip on water management. Watch the momentum of loss.

******

Here and there. Then and now. The intersection is constantly shifting, and this is the line Bruce walks with his images. Where he grew up, the rural roads and farm parcels still hold memories of his ten-year-old self, but the land itself has vastly changed over the past fifty years. The wild and silent rock faces, the looming mountain peaks of the remote valley where he lives now (and which will be the subject of Volume II, forthcoming), seem to still be owned by the earth. You can look out for miles and it's a view that could have been seen one hundred years ago. Perhaps that this rare corner of the state is characteristically rooted in its own ancient memory is what drew him here, to land, to build a home in his adult years.

You can look at images from these bodies of work—Bruce's photographic explorations of his past and his present—and see through his eyes the same gray sky, a similar narrative of forgetting and remembering. The wistful bend of winter tree limbs arc like hard memories, the kind from our childhood we try to forget but can't. Panning out across the San Joaquin Valley traveling 65 mph along highway 198 or 33 or 41 (where Bruce's father Ernie Haley had the auto accident that took his life), the pumpjacks, the trash piled up in places, the abandoned buildings, and even the path of power lines alter the view. Things change in this life. Sometimes they break and can't be put back together again. But the haze and rose-tinged light, the bluffs off in the distance, the endless dirt roads you'll find if you peel off the main and follow the tire tracks to somewhere...all of that remains year after dusty year.

Dairies stand empty or are in the process of being demolished. The basketball hoop standing like a sentinel is missing its net. A puddle of water accumulated at the shoulder mirrors the sky, as if asking for rain. Wouldn't matter if the clouds dumped for days. Water resource management is embedded and embroiled in policies that are often described as labyrinthine, and that have knotted up on themselves for decades. You pull on one thread, and it only tightens another: surface water, groundwater, aquifer, pumping, land subsidence.

So, hopeless? No. But you cannot hide from the past.